Rob Eastaway

Illustrated by
Nikalas Catlow

Published in the UK in 2007 by Wizard Books,
an imprint of Icon Books Ltd., The Old Dairy,
Brook Road, Thriplow, Cambridge SG8 7RG
email: wizard@iconbooks.co.uk
www.iconbooks.co.uk/wizard

First published by Element Children's Books in 1999

Sold in the UK, Europe, South Africa and Asia by
Faber and Faber Ltd., 3 Queen Square, London WC1N 3AU
or their agents

Distributed in the UK, Europe, South Africa and Asia by
TBS Ltd., TBS Distribution Centre, Colchester Road,
Frating Green, Colchester CO7 7DW

Published in Australia in 2007 by
Allen & Unwin Pty. Ltd., PO Box 8500,
83 Alexander Street, Crows Nest, NSW 2065

Distributed in Canada by Penguin Books Canada,
90 Eglinton Avenue East, Suite 700, Toronto, Ontario M4P 2Y3

ISBN-10: 1-84046-797-5
ISBN-13: 978-1840467-97-0

View of a Pig by Ted Hughes printed
with the kind permission of Faber and Faber Ltd.,
The Termite and *The Camel* by Ogden Nash printed
with the kind permission of Curtis Brown Ltd. (USA)
and Andre Deutsch (UK)

Typesetting by Wayzgoose

Printed in the UK by CPI Bookmarque, Croydon, CR0 4TD

Acknowledgements

I would like to thank my nephews Tom and Mark, who enthusiastically helped me with several of the experiments, my encyclopaedic researchers David and Ian who dug up some memorable material, and Hazel and Barry for steering me in the right direction. Thanks also to Martha and Dave, Peter and Mary, Chris and the 'Good Old Days?' group. I'm also indebted to the teachers and children at St John The Baptist National School Midleton, the American School of Bucharest, Lakeside School Coppell and Nation's Ford Charlotte for all their help in testing out the experiments. And thank you Elaine for your support and encouragement throughout.

Thanks also to Tom Lorenzin, Barbara Abrahams, Helen Nicol and everyone else I quizzed over several months.

R.E.

Contents

Part Two

Part Three

Introduction

Inside you is one of the most incredible computers on Earth. It has the ability to store billions of bits of information and to retrieve them in almost no time at all. It can instantly recognise a noise or a smell, handwriting or a picture, much faster and more reliably than electronic computers.

What is this computer? It is your brain, of course. The human brain is so clever and so complicated, it is only in recent years that we have begun to understand how it works and what it can do.

Of all the skills a brain has, one of the most important and the most mysterious is memory.

What is memory? How does it work? Do animals have memories? Is it possible to remember everything?

Can ordinary people improve their memories so that they become super-powerful? These are some of the mysteries that we shall be investigating.

In Part One of the book you can explore different ways of remembering and discover how to make the most of your brain. In Part Two, you can find out what scientists have discovered about the way that memory and the brain work. Part Three contains 50 fun and easy-to-learn memory aids that will give you instant recall to all kinds of useful facts and information to impress your friends.

Throughout the book there are some amazing true stories about memory to read and exciting tasks and experiments to do.

So if you are all set for an exciting brain adventure, read on!

PART ONE

How to Remember More

Did you know that according to some experts people make use of less than 10 per cent of their brain? In fact, some have even claimed that we use only 1 per cent. If this is true, then you have the potential to make a huge improvement to your memory. This section gives you the chance to test this out. There are lots of tips and techniques for improving your memory. But watch out! Any new technique takes time to learn. Allow yourself the chance to practise, and then who knows? Maybe you will discover that you have some powers that will really surprise you. Let's start off with an experiment.

Experiment 1 – Which Words?

On page 12 is a list of 20 words. Read it once and then turn back to this page. DO IT NOW!

OK, have you done it? Now write down as many words from the list as you can. How many can you remember?

_____   _____

_____   _____

_____   _____

_____   _____

_____   _____

_____   _____

_____   _____

_____   _____

_____   _____

_____   _____

If you got five you have done very well. The important thing is which words you remembered. It is common for people to remember the first and last items in a list, so perhaps you remembered 'Doll' and 'Bed'. One word that you almost certainly remembered was 'Zippedy-Doo-Dah'. Why? Because it was bigger and sillier than all the others in the list. Brains are especially good at remembering unusual or silly things.

READ THE LIST ONCE THEN TURN BACK THE PAGE

Doll
Hand
Green
Two
Plastic
Fell
Stick
Zippedy-Doo-Da!
Gum
Bucket
Fly
Speed
Heavy
Floor
High
Cook
Time
How
Angry
Bed

Creating a Story

One reason why you didn't remember everything on the list is that there is no connection between the words. It is much harder to remember things that are jumbled than things that have connections and a pattern. Test this for yourself. Here are two patterns made with matchsticks. Look at both for a few seconds and then cover them up. Which do you remember best?

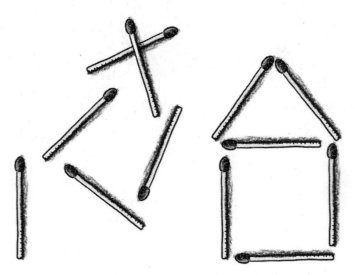

Both patterns are made with six matches, but the one on the right is easier to remember because it makes a recognisable shape. Each match connects clearly to the next. Memory works best when the things you are trying to remember link together.

One way to link a list is with a story. Let's try this with the list of words on the previous page and make up a story using all of them. Don't forget, the sillier the story, the easier it will be to remember!

Once there was a PLASTIC DOLL with TWO GREEN HANDS. One hand FELL off, so I had to STICK it back on with GUM. 'ZIPPEDY-DOO-DA!' I said, 'I wonder if it will FLY?' But it was too HEAVY and it landed in a BUCKET on the FLOOR at HIGH SPEED. 'HOW did this happen?' said the ANGRY COOK. 'It is TIME for BED!'

Read the story again, then cover it up and see how much you can recall. You will probably find that you remember more of the words in the list this way. Next time you have an important list to remember, why not link everything on it with a story?

It's useful for remembering ...

What to take to school

Shopping lists

Spellings for a test

The players in your favourite team

Phone messages

The names of your classmates

Memory by story-telling

During the last hundred years, explorers of remote parts of the world found many tribes where there was no tradition of writing things down. All of the stories and legends of the tribe were passed from one generation to the next by story-tellers who held all of the information in their heads. Anthropologists who recorded these stories sometimes found that a story-teller had memorized so much that it took him six days to recite it all. Written down it would be enough to fill hundreds of pages. How did they learn these stories? Almost certainly by listening and repeating again and again until they were perfect. Repetition is a powerful way to remember!

The story method is very good for remembering some types of lists, but it won't help you to remember everything. For example, if you moved to a new school, how would you remember the names of everyone in your new class?

Well, you could try out a method that was discovered over 2,000 years ago by an ancient Greek poet called Simonides.

The Story of Simonides

The poet Simonides was often asked to recite his poetry in front of an audience. One day, he was hired as the after-dinner entertainment at a banquet given by a nobleman called Scopas. Simonides had written a special poem for Scopas and recited it to the guests. Two messengers then arrived to see him so, immediately after he finished reciting, Simonides left the building. While he was outside, a terrible disaster struck.

There was a sudden earthquake and the whole building collapsed, squashing everyone inside. The guests at the banquet were reduced to a horrible, gooey mess and it was impossible to tell who was who. This was a big problem because the families of those inside needed to know which body was which. Fortunately, Simonides was able to remember exactly who was who by picturing their positions around the dining table.

This gave Simonides an idea. He realised that it had been easy to remember the guests because they had all been in certain places around the room. Simonides used his experience at the banquet to invent a clever way of memorizing, which he called 'The Room Method'.

Using Simonides at school

Try to think of everyone in your class without missing anyone out. Do you find that difficult? Simonides' room method might help you to remember. Think of the tables in your classroom with everyone seated in their usual places. As you look from table to table, you can probably picture which person in your class sits there. So, to remember everyone in your class, all you have to do is make a mind picture of the tables. Does it work for you?

The Room Method

In ancient Greece, memory was one of the most important subjects learnt at school and university. Many pupils were taught Simonides' room method of remembering. Here is a chance to try the ancient room method and see if it helps you to remember a shopping list.

Before you start, look at the picture of the room below containing eight labelled objects. Test yourself to make sure you can remember where each object goes.

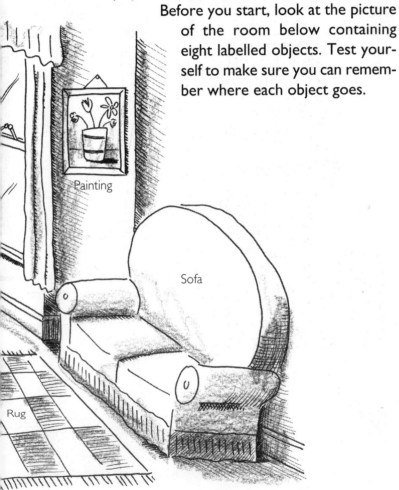

Painting

Sofa

Rug

Now, here is a shopping list of eight items to memorize. You are going to remember each one by connecting it to the memory room.

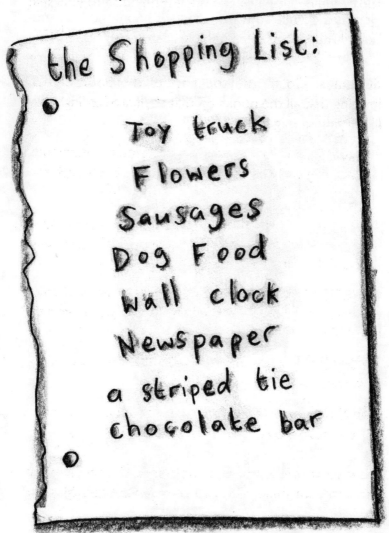

the Shopping List:

Toy truck
Flowers
Sausages
Dog Food
Wall clock
Newspaper
a striped tie
chocolate bar

Let's remember these objects in a particular way.

Toy truck: Imagine that a toy truck is running along the top of the radiator – make the engine noise to yourself!

Flowers: Look at the TV. Imagine that there are beautiful flowers on the screen.

Sausages: Go to the top row of the bookshelves. Imagine that all the books on that shelf are sizzling away like frying sausages.

Dog food: Look at the window. Imagine an enormous dog holding a can of dog food is peering in through the window.

Wall clock: Imagine that the hook holding up the painting is the second hand on a clock, slowly ticking around – tick, tick, tick …

Newspaper: Imagine that a newspaper is draped over the back of the sofa – it crinkles up every time you sit back!

Striped tie: Imagine that the pattern on the rug is made of striped ties.

Chocolate bar: Imagine that a bar of chocolate is melting and oozing over the table.

Now close the book and look around the memory room in your mind. Can you remember everything on the list?

So how did you get on? It is usual to get a score of at least five out of eight when you use this method. If you didn't get all eight, think about why. It may have been that the images you made in your head weren't clear enough. It helps if the images are really silly, even moving around and making noises — for example, a snarling dog looking through the window, tapping at the pane with the can!

Word perfect

In ancient Greece, politicians and lawyers often had to give speeches. There was sometimes a rule that the speaker was not allowed to use any written notes — just imagine how difficult that would be! To learn their speeches, the Greeks used the room method. They would store different parts of a speech in different parts of a 'memory house'. They would then imagine walking through the house, picking up bits of the speech as they went.

The room method caught on in Rome, too. Julius Caesar probably used it when he gave his great speeches. Memory was especially important for military leaders because they needed to know the names of their soldiers. One of the great Roman generals, Publius Scipio, was said to have known the names of every one of his 35,000 soldiers. How many names do you know?

A Party Trick!

Before television was invented, families had to find other ways to entertain themselves. Many families had a piano at home, and on Sunday evenings they would often sing songs together. They would also play games or perform party tricks. Memory tricks were popular – children would often recite poems forwards and backwards for their parents!

One popular memory trick was for a person to learn a list of 16 words and then repeat them in whatever order the audience chose. For example, he or she might be asked: 'What was number 12?' or 'Name every other word on the list.'

You can do this trick using the room method to help you. To remember a list of 16 objects, use each piece of furniture in the memory room for remembering two things. For example, use the bookshelves to remember sausages and ketchup. Imagine the bottom shelf holding sausages sizzling away, and the top shelf holding ketchup, ready to be poured all over them.

To remember exactly where an object comes in your list, remember the objects in your room in this order:

1 Radiator
2 Radiator pipes
3 TV screen
4 TV aerial
5 Top bookshelf
6 Bottom bookshelf

7   Window
8   Curtains
9   Picture hook
10 Picture
11 Sofa back
12 Sofa cushions
13 The pattern on the rug
14 The fringe around the rug
15 The table top
16 The underside of the table

To memorize the 16 objects on the list, move around the room and 'leave' each object on a piece of furniture. When you are quizzed, first picture the correct part of the room, then 'look' to see what you left there. For example, object number 8 on the list will be on the curtains.

A group of ten-year-olds and I tested this out using two different lists. We memorized the first list by reading it through in the ordinary way. For the second list, we used the memory room method. One boy, Matt, had the most spectacular results. He scored 4 using the normal system, but 16 with the room method!

You will find that most of the things in the list stick in your mind for at least an hour and sometimes for as long as a day or a week. You can use the memory room in this book or you can create your own. It can be a real room, such as your bedroom or classroom, or you can draw your own.

'S' the Amazing Memory Man

With practice, the room method can help you to memorize far more information than you ever thought possible. Even so, you are unlikely to be able to match the most amazing memory man of all time. His name was Shereskevskii who was born in Russia in the late 1800s. Shereskevskii, who became known simply as 'S', was a newspaper reporter when his amazing memory was discovered. One morning, the editor of the newspaper was briefing his journalists when he noticed that S wasn't taking any notes. When the editor accused him of not paying attention, S repeated, word for word, the instructions he had been given. The editor was astonished, but S had no idea that what he was doing was anything unusual.

A scientist called Alexander Luria tested S's memory. To Luria's amazement, S was able to repeat every set of numbers and words that he was given. However difficult Luria made the tests, S never made a mistake. Luria studied S for 30 years with some astonishing results. Sometimes he would ask S to recall a test he had given him 15 years earlier.

'What was the test I gave you in 1929?' he asked one day in 1944. S thought for a moment before replying, 'Yes, this was a test you gave me in your apartment sitting at the table, I in the rocking chair, you wearing a dark suit, I can see you saying "1, 13, 74, 29".'

Luria was fascinated to know how S pulled off this amazing memory stunt. S explained the extraordinary way that his mind worked. The first thing was that he

remembered everything as pictures. If he had a list of objects to memorize, he would begin by imagining himself in a familiar place, such as the street where he lived. He would then 'go for a walk' in his street, and as he passed something that was familiar such as his front door, he would 'attach' to it the item he had to remember. So, if he needed to remember a duck, a loaf of bread and a book, he would 'see' a duck on his front door, a loaf of bread on the next front step and a bible at the street corner. In fact, he had invented a memory system just like the room method of Simonides!

His picture system also worked for numbers, which he always saw as pictures. For example, when asked to think of the number 2, he imagined a dark rectangle.

S only ever forgot anything when he put an object in a place where it was hard to see. Once he forgot 'egg' because, in his mind, he had put it next to a white wall so he couldn't see it. He also forgot 'shoe' because it was hidden in a dark corner of his street, but he solved that problem by adding a streetlight!

S could even remember being a baby. He was able to picture his mother looking down on him in his cot and recall the feeling of comfort on hearing her voice. As a child, he had such a powerful imagination that he lived a kind of fantasy life. Sometimes, he would wake up in the morning thinking: 'Oh I don't want to go to school – I'll imagine that somebody else has gone instead of me.' He would then be so convinced that this had really happened that he would go back to sleep – only for his dad to find him and shout: 'What are you doing in bed?! You should have gone to school by now!'.

When he grew up, S found it difficult to settle into a job. In the end, he found the perfect career as a memory man and performed in theatres all over the country. Unfortunately, S's biggest problem was that he found it very hard to forget anything. At the end of each performance he was left exhausted and confused. Finally, he taught himself how to forget by mentally covering up all the things he didn't want to remember with a huge sheet. If he couldn't see them, they disappeared from his memory!

Remembering Numbers

The memory room system is good for remembering lists of objects or people's faces, but it isn't a good method for memorizing numbers.

One of the best ways to remember numbers was invented in about 1730 by Dr Richard Grey, who was very interested in the way in which the mind works. His research had shown that people often had problems remembering numbers and found it much easier to remember words. You can test this for yourself:

Experiment 2 – Numbers or Words?

Which are easier to remember – the numbers or the words?

5 7 8 1 4 1 2 0   or   *'Look, a fat rat in a zoo'*

6 3 8 9 2 1 4 5 3 2   or   *'Jim Fop ain't a real man'*

Study each one for a few seconds, then test yourself. Like Dr Grey, you probably found the phrases much easier to remember than the numbers. This is because the words mean something.

Dr Grey's idea was to find a way of turning numbers into words. In his system, each digit is turned into a certain letter of the alphabet and the letters are then turned into words. In fact, this is exactly the case with the experiment just now!

Before you can use the numbers to letters system, you need to learn the following list, in which each number is linked to a letter:

How to Remember

1 is **T**   **T** has *one* line going down

2 is **N**   **N** has *two* feet

3 is **M**   **M** has *three* feet

4 is **R**   **R** is the *fourth* letter of fouR

5 is **L**   **L** is the Roman number for 50

6 is **J**   6 is something like a backwards **J**

7 is **K**   **K** is like two figure 7s joined together

8 is **F**   An old-fashioned squiggly **f** looks like an 8

9 is **P**   9 is like a backwards **P**

0 is **Z**   **Z** is for Zero

Remember this list by writing it out a few times and asking a friend to test you. Carry on until it has stuck. It shouldn't take you long.

Now, use the list to help you memorize a number. Suppose that you need to remember the security code 5 7 6 3 for entry into a building. First, turn the numbers into letters:

5 7 6 3 is **L K J M**

Now think of words containing the letters in this order. If you can, make the words (or word) connect with the subject – exact spelling doesn't matter. For example, you might think of

LoKJaM

That should be easy to remember – you can imagine that the lock is jammed and you can't open it! Once you have learnt the words, change the letters back into the number every time you use it:

L is 5, K is 7, J is 6 and M is 3

Have you noticed that the vowels don't count? It is only the letters you learnt that matter.

Another way to remember **L K J M** would be to make up a silly phrase, such as:

'Love Keeping Jelly Monsters'

This is so silly that it is bound to stick in your mind! Use this system and you will quickly become extremely good at remembering numbers.

This method will also help you to memorize famous dates. For example, Henry VIII became King of England in 1509.

The numbers 1509 are T L Z P.

You could remember this by imagining King Henry with a Tail fastened by a Zip:

'Henry VIII Tail Zip'

It sounds silly, but it is easy to remember!

Experiment 3 – Remembering Dates

Use the word method to learn these famous years. You can ignore the first number – 'I' – as this begins nearly every well-known year. Try inventing your own ways of remembering before looking at the suggestions further down and on the next page.

1927 The year in which American aviator Charles Lindbergh made the first flight across the Atlantic Ocean.

1815 The year of the Battle of Waterloo, when French Emperor Napoleon was defeated by the English.

The Suggestions

(1)-9-2-7 Lindbergh

Think of words that contain **P(9) – N(2) – K(7)**, such as **PiNK**.

Picture Lindbergh flying in a **PiNK** aeroplane.

(1)-8-1-5 Waterloo

Think of words with the letters F(8) – T(1) – L(5). How about FaTaL? Battles are often FaTaL for the soldiers, so…

Imagine Waterloo as a FaTaL battle.

Another suggestion is:

'FaT Lemons'

Imagine a row of FaT Lemons lining up to fight at Waterloo!

Now it is easy to see what Experiment 2 was for. The two phrases you found it easy to remember were actually the same as the numbers you found it difficult to remember!

'LooK, a FaT RaT iN a Zoo.'
5 7   8 1 4 1 2 0

'JiM FoP aiN'T a ReaL MaN.'
6 3 8 9   2 1   4   5 3   2

Adding More Letters

If you want to use more of the letters for the number system, you can add to the earlier list. Here is the full set:

1 is **T** or **D**
(D sounds like T – same tongue position for both)

2 is **N**

3 is **M**

4 is **R**

5 is **L**

6 is **J** or **CH** or **SH**
(Same tongue position for all three)

7 is **K** or **C** or **G** or **Q**
(Same mouth positions, almost identical sounds)

8 is **F** or **PH** or **V**
(Same lip positions, almost identical sounds)

9 is **P** or **B**
(Same lip position)

0 is **Z** or **S**
(Same tongue position)

This gives plenty of letters for making up words. For example, 'Go To BeD' would be **7191**.

It's useful for remembering ...

Phone numbers

Security codes

Famous dates

House numbers

Memorizing with Rhymes

Experiment 4 – Remembering Poems

Here are two poems. Which one do you remember best?

View of a Pig

The pig lay on a barrow dead
He weighed, they said, as much as three men
Its eyes closed, pink white eyelashes
Its trotters stuck straight out.

Or

The Termite

A hungry termite tapped on wood
And tasted it and found it good
And that is why your Auntie May
Fell through the kitchen floor today!

Most people find the second poem much easier to remember than the first. Do you? There are *three* things about *The Termite* poem that makes it more memorable:

• It has a simple rhythm. Try humming the termite poem with closed lips. You should hear a regular 'mmm MMM mmm MMM mmm MMM mmm MMM' running all the way through it. The pig poem has a less regular rhythm.

- The termite poem has a funny ending. If you laughed at it, you probably found it stuck in your mind.

- The lines rhyme with each other. The brain likes hearing rhymes which is why so many advertising slogans have rhymes in them, such as:

'A Mars a day – helps you work, rest and play'

That catchy slogan was used to sell Mars bars for years.

Simple, rhythmic poems are one of the best ways of making something memorable. Lots of memory aids have been invented using rhymes. Do you remember the date that Columbus sailed across the Atlantic?

In Fourteen hundred and ninety-two
Columbus sailed the ocean blue!

Or, have you heard of the old saying that advises you to avoid future mistakes?

A stitch in time
Saves nine

If you need to remember something, such as getting home by 4.30pm, see if you can make it into a rhyme with an easy rhythm:

If I don't get home by half-past four
Dad will have gone and locked the door!

Picking up a Pattern

Numbers and shapes are much easier to remember if you can spot a pattern. Imagine that you are a spy and you have been passed a secret computer code for getting into a confidential computer file. Can you memorize it?

Secret code: 1 1 1 5 1 9 2 3 2 7 3 1 3 5

Unless you can spot a pattern, you will find it difficult to learn. Can you see the pattern? Try to find it before you look at the answer below. Here is the code again:

11 15 19 23 27 31 35

Now can you see the pattern? It is a series of numbers increasing by four each time. Once you have spotted this, the code is easy to remember.

Here is another, trickier test. Look at these nine symbols. How quickly can you remember them?

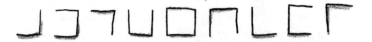

Difficult isn't it! Now here is a way to memorize them instantly. First, draw a grid for a game of Noughts and Crosses.

Now start at the top left-hand corner and go down each column in turn. Do you recognise the shapes? To remember the nine symbols, all you have to do is to imagine the Noughts and Crosses grid and go down each column.

Sometimes you can only spot patterns if you are an expert. Look at these two chessboards. Which one do you think you would find it easier to remember?

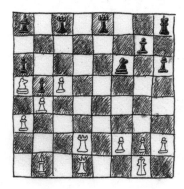 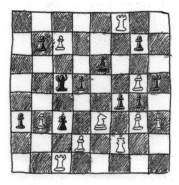

You may find them equally difficult. But to an expert chess player, the one on the left is much easier to remember. This is because the arrangement on the left could really happen in a game. The one on the right is complete nonsense, however, and could never happen in a serious match.

A knight to remember!

Chess players have performed some amazing feats of memory. American chess player Bobby Fisher memorized the details of every big chess match ever played by one of his chess heroes, Alexander Alekhine.

In 1977 the Hungarian chess player James Flesch played 52 games of chess simultaneously while blindfolded. Unable to see any of the boards, he had to picture the position of each game in his head. Incidentally, the former USSR top chess players were forbidden from giving simultaneous displays of chess like this because of the mental strain that it caused them!

Using Your Senses

Not everyone thinks or remembers in the same way. Some people learn by repeating words to themselves – they need to have heard the sound of a word in order to remember it. Others need to be able to see things written down and yet other people rely on touch. Test this for yourself with the breakfast experiment.

Experiment 5 – What did you have for breakfast?

Think about what you had for breakfast this morning. Describe it out loud, as accurately as you can – close your eyes if you want to. Do it now before you read on!

Answer these questions (you will probably answer 'no' to some):

Did you SEE pictures of breakfast in your mind?

YES/NO

Did you make SOUND EFFECTS as you re-created your breakfast?   YES/NO

Did you FEEL what your breakfast was like – its crunchiness, how it felt on your tongue?   YES/NO

Did you think about the SMELL?   YES/NO

Did you MOVE AROUND or use your hands as you were remembering your breakfast?   YES/NO

Which came first in your mind:

SEEING, FEELING, HEARING or SMELLING?

You probably answered 'yes' to the first question, because the most common way to remember anything is through pictures. However, some people remember mainly through sounds, while others remember through touch and sensations. The people with the best memories probably combine all their senses!

Have you ever walked into a room, breathed in the smell of the furniture, and immediately been reminded of something?

'Wow, this reminds me of Grandma's house', or 'This makes me think of the time we went to stay in that old hotel.'

Although people usually remember by seeing pictures in their minds, the sense that has the closest link with memory is smell. This is because the place where the smell sensors connect to the brain is very close to the place where memory is controlled.

Scientists have even found that your sense of smell can help you to pass exams! They carried out an experiment where a group of children learnt in a classroom scented with a particular smell. The exam room was then scented with the same smell. These children's exam results turned out to be better than the group whose classroom had been unscented. Do you think familiar scents would help you to pass an exam? If you want to use the smell technique yourself, remember to ask your teacher first!

The Rat Man

The famous psychologist Sigmund Freud had a patient called the 'Rat Man' (so called because of his fear of rats) who could recognise everyone he knew by their smell. Many people would understand how this is possible. Perfume makers, for example, use their well-developed sense of smell to help them distinguish between hundreds of scents, while some mothers can recognize which are their children's T-shirts just by their smell.

Photographic Memory

There is one rare but very special type of memory known as photographic memory. There is a series of detective stories in which a girl called Cam Jansen says 'Click!' as she memorizes information, while in the film *Carry On Spying*, there is a spy who 'photographs' documents by closing her eyes and making the clicking sound of a camera!

All this sounds amazing, but does it actually happen like this? People with true photographic memories may not click when taking in information, but they can certainly store enormous amounts of detail as 'mind pictures' in their brains. It is also a fact that children are usually better at this than adults. A photographic memory is probably best described as a good visual memory.

Real-life spies need to store information in their heads because carrying documents is too dangerous. Around the time of the Second World War, a master Russian spy, Richard Sorge, worked undercover as a journalist in Japan. All the while, he was secretly getting hold of Japanese intelligence information and feeding it back to his own country. He would quickly memorize documents and messages and then destroy them (often by eating them!) so that there was no shred of evidence left.

Artists often have great visual memories. The famous British 19th-century landscape painter J. W. Turner often went fishing, and this was the time when ideas and impressions for his paintings would form. Back in his studio, he relied heavily on his powerful memory to create his vivid pictures.

It is likely that YOU have a powerful memory for pictures. In one scientific test, a group of people were shown 2,500 photographs with only a few seconds to look at each picture. The group was then shown 280 pairs of pictures and asked to recall which of the pair they had seen before. The average score was 250 out of 280! With only one second to look at each picture, most people remembered almost every one they had previously seen.

The ability to remember people's faces is even more extraordinary. It is thought that a normal person can recognise up to 10,000 different ones!

Photographic memory was the key!

A young prisoner in England memorized the exact size and shape of the keys to the prison locks after seeing them for no more than a few seconds. He then cut up a plastic mirror and made exact copies! When the keys were discovered, the prison officers had to change all of the locks in the prison. They also had to ensure that they didn't let the young prisoner catch the slightest glimpse of their keys again!

Musical Memory

If you ever find yourself humming a tune after you have been listening to the radio or a CD, then you will know that you have a musical memory. Of all the memories that stick in your brain, music seems to stay there the longest. Perhaps this is why musical jingles are as popular in adverts as rhymes! In the film *The Lady Vanishes* by Alfred Hitchcock, a spy passed on a message as a tune. Well, it must be simpler than needing a photographic memory!

Many people have incredible musical memories. When the great composer Mozart was 14 he heard a piece of church music called *Miserere* for the first time. It had been composed for a particular choir and never written down. After hearing it only once, Mozart was able to reproduce it perfectly, note for note!

People who suffer from Alzheimer's disease slowly forget everything – even the names of people in their family. The very last things that they remember are often the songs and tunes that they learnt when they were young. This shows just how strong the memory of music is.

So good he did it in his sleep!

There is a remarkable true story about a concert pianist who fell asleep at the keyboard during a performance. To the audience's amazement, the sleeping pianist continued to play the piece perfectly right to the very end when he woke up.

Some pianists believe that some of their memory must be stored in their fingers.

Memory Triggers

Not all memories return on demand. Some memories come back in a sudden, unexpected flash. Usually, these memories are triggered by something else, such as an object, a smell or a picture.

In fact, some memories will only come back when something linked to that memory is present. A 17th-century Englishman called John Locke wrote about a man who was able to dance only when a trunk was in the room. The reason for this was that the man had *learnt* to dance in a room with a trunk in it. He seemed incapable of dancing if there was no trunk there.

Location can have a big effect on your memory. If you learn spellings for a test in your bedroom, then the place where you are most likely to remember them is … your bedroom. But if you then take some familiar objects from your bedroom with you when you do the test, it is possible that they can trigger your memory.

The connection between location and learning was once tested in a very strange experiment. Six divers were each given a list of 40 words to remember. They learnt 20 words on shore and 20 under water. Then they were tested, once on land and once under water. The words they had learnt under the water were recalled better under water than on land, while the words they had learnt on land were better remembered on shore.

Occasionally, memories struggle to return. There are times when you are asked a question and you are sure that you know the answer but you just can't think of it.

'It's on the tip of my tongue!' or 'Don't tell me, don't tell me, I've almost got it!'

When this happens, the tiniest hints or prompts can help you to recall what you need to remember.

Experiment 6 – Letter Clues

Answer the following questions as well as you can. For the ones you can't quite remember, see if the single letter after the question jogs your memory.

1	What is the longest river in the world?	**N**
2	What is a female fox called?	**V**
3	What colour comes after green and blue in a rainbow?	**I**

4 Which mountain range is Mount Everest in? **H**

5 Which film is the biggest box office hit of all time? **T**

6 What do you call a group of lions? **P**

7 What is a baby swan called? **C**

8 What was the second dinosaur period called? **J**

9 Which large bird became extinct about 300 years ago? **D**

10 What do you call a shape with five sides the same length? **P**

Did the initials help you to answer some of the questions? If you are trying hard to remember somebody's name, it can help to go through each letter of the alphabet in turn. When you get to the right initial, your brain will often leap into action and recall the name you are looking for.

Not all memories are stored in the brain. Most people have photo albums or videos to remind them of their family, friends and special occasions. Others keep diaries, and nearly everyone returns from a trip or visit with a souvenir. All these objects are part of your memory, like an extension to your brain.

Answers to the quiz: 1 Nile 2 Vixen 3 Indigo 4 Himalayas 5 Titanic 6 Pride 7 Cygnet 8 Jurassic 9 Dodo 10 Pentagon

How much memory do you keep in your bedroom?

Have a look around your bedroom. How many of the things in your room are linked to memories? You probably have holiday mementoes – perhaps a picture, a T-shirt, a stick of rock or a toy. The purpose of these is to give your memory a helping hand.

'Souvenir' is a French word meaning 'to remember', and 'memento' comes from the Latin word for memory.

Invent Your Own Mnemonics

A great way to remember facts is by using what are known as mnemonics (say nee-monics), named after Mnemosyne, the Greek goddess of memory. A mnemonic is a rhyme, saying or special trick that helps you to remember.

Suppose you want to learn the names of the world's six longest rivers, which are:

> **Nile**
> **Amazon**
> **Mississippi**
> **Yangtze**
> **Yellow**
> **Amur**

The initials are: **N A M Y Y A**

This could become 'Next August My Yellow Yacht Arrives', or even 'Nipping Ants Make You Yell Aloud!'

Now it's your turn. Make up a mnemonic to help you remember the four biggest moons around the planet Jupiter (which is a big, cold planet): Ganymede, Io, Callisto, Europa. Write it here:

Medical students have to learn lots of facts about the human body. To help them, they learn lots of mnemonics. Medical mnemonics are often very silly because then they are easier to remember! For example, this is the mnemonic they use to remember which nerves in the spine control the bowels:

S 2 3 4
Keeps your guts off the floor!

Just imagine your doctor saying that!

Fantastic memory feat

Bartholomew Parker Bidder worked in the customer records department of a large insurance company. One day, a huge fire swept through the building and destroyed most of the files. This could have been a disaster, but the amazing Mr Bidder was able to reconstruct them all from memory! This incredible feat took him 6 months.

Memory Games

Most scientists believe that, just like the rest of the body, the brain stays healthy through exercise. A good way to give your brain a workout is to play memory games. Here are four games you can try out with your friends.

Kim's Game

About 20 different objects are arranged on a tray. The players study the tray for two minutes before it is covered up. Everyone has one minute to write down the objects they can remember. The winner is the person who remembers the most. (If you play this using the room method you have a good chance of winning.)

Chinese Whispers

This is not a contest, but it is great fun. Everyone sits around in a circle. The first player thinks of a message – it could be: 'My Aunt Clarissa has a Siamese cat.' He or she then whispers it to the person next to them, who then whispers it to the next person and so on, until it reaches the last person in the circle. The last person then repeats the message they heard out loud. Usually it is completely different! For example, the message about Aunt Clarissa once ended up as: 'Five part misser as I am an idiot.'

There is a famous story in which an English general sent an urgent message to his headquarters. It was, 'Send reinforcements, we're going to advance.' As it passed from person to person, the message got changed to 'Send three and four pence, we're going to a dance' – and three and four pence is all the general received!

I Went on Holiday

This is a great game for between five and ten players. Everyone must sit around in a circle and the first player begins: 'I went on holiday and I took (for example) some sunglasses.' The next person says: 'I went on holiday and I took some sunglasses and a camera.' Each player has to remember every item listed so far, and then add one new one on to the end. Anyone who makes a mistake has to drop out and sit outside the circle.

This makes it harder for everyone else because, without realising it, they were using the missing person's face as a trigger to remember their objects. The winner of the game is the last one to be left in the circle.

Matching Pairs

The aim of this game, for two or more players, is to collect as many cards as possible by remembering where the pairs are. Shuffle an ordinary pack of cards and spread them all face down on a table or the floor. The first player turns over two cards. If they are the same number or picture, he or she keeps the pair and has another go at turning over two cards. If they don't match, the player puts them back face down in exactly the same places. Then it is the second player's turn. The winner is the player who finishes with the highest number of pairs.

Juggling act

One memory expert in southern India once performed a kind of mental juggling act when he showed that it is possible for the brain to keep track of several things at once. While playing a chess game (without seeing the board) he answered general knowledge questions, learnt a verse of poetry, kept count of how many times a bell was rung, memorized two lines of Spanish and did calculations in his head.

More Memory Tips

The author of the first complete English dictionary, Dr Johnson, once said, 'The true art of memory is the art of attention.' He meant that if your mind isn't concentrating properly, then you won't remember anything. This experiment explains it perfectly:

Experiment 7 – Tele(re)vision?

Switch on the TV and turn to something that interests you. Then, spend two minutes trying to memorize this list of ten words:

Box	Crane
Car	Pig
Door	Shelf
Helter Skelter	Raincoat
Wasp	Tree

Can you concentrate on the TV and still learn all ten words? Test yourself. Try learning ten different words with the TV switched off. Was it easier? Most people find that their performance is much worse when they are distracted than when they are able to concentrate.

Concentrating and paying attention take a lot of effort. Some teachers use a very curious method for getting pupils to concentrate while they are learning.

As a teacher asks a question, he or she will throw a ball to the student. This method is said to produce more correct answers because it relaxes the mind and frees the memory! What do you think? Try it out with a friend or suggest it to your teacher.

Some people find words difficult to remember. Think about the breakfast experiment on page 41. You may have found that you think best in pictures, sounds or sensations. If it is pictures, you can improve your learning by drawing diagrams of whatever you need to remember. If sounds work for you, say the words out loud to yourself, exaggerate them and even add sound effects. If you remember sensations best, move around as you are memorizing and imagine the texture of the objects you are remembering.

You need a good memory to be an actor. For some

roles, actors have to learn as much as 50 pages of lines. How do they do it? The answer is that instead of trying to learn a whole play at once, actors spend a short time learning just two or three pages. Once they are certain they know a chunk thoroughly, they take a break before beginning to learn the next few pages.

So, if you have lots to remember, you will learn better by breaking it up into, say, an hour a day spread over three days, than a single, tiring three-hour session.

One final tip to help you remember: sometimes, the harder you try to remember something, the more difficult it gets. If you find that you really can't remember, say to yourself:

> *'I have to remember where I left my ruler and I know it will come to me in a moment.'*

Then start doing something entirely different and, very often, you will find that the memory will suddenly pop up in your head!

Experiment 8 – Looking and Observing

Over the page is a picture of a clock. Have a good look at it, then turn back. DO IT NOW! Can you remember what the number four looked like on the clock? Write it here:

_____

You probably remembered that the numbers on the clock were Roman numerals. Did you think that the four looked like this?:

IV

If you look at the clock again, you will see that it actually says **IIII**. In fact if you look at ANY clock with Roman numbers on it, it almost certainly has four written as **IIII**. No matter how often you have looked at a clock, you may not have noticed this. You see what you want to see, not what is actually there. This is the difference between looking and observing. Observing is seeing what is really there!

Super-Powerful Memories

You now know that there are lots of methods you can use to improve your memory. Some people use these techniques to develop super-powerful memories. Every year, a world memory championship is held where contestants are set all sorts of challenges, such as:

- Memorizing the position of every card in a shuffled pack

- Learning a long string of numbers

- Remembering hundreds of names and faces

The champions use techniques that are very similar to those you've tried out in this book. Some use a version of the story method, others prefer to rely on the room method, or choose a numbers-to-words system. The method they choose depends on what they have to remember. So now that you know the secrets, do you think that YOU have the ability to create your own super-powerful memory?

Pi-eyed

Some feats of memory have been completely useless – except to get people into the record books. In Tokyo in 1995, Hiroyuki Goto memorized the number pi (3.14159) to 42,195 decimal places! This took him hours. Just to show what a mind-numbing task this must have been, here are the first 100 digits that he had to learn:

3.14159265358979323846264338327950288419716939937510582097494459230781640628620899862803482534211170679

PART TWO

How Memory Works

Have you ever wondered how important your memory is to you? If you had no memory, you would think that you were experiencing everything for the very first time. If you looked in a mirror, you would wonder who you were and you wouldn't have an idea what your name was. Not only this, as you stood looking at yourself in the mirror you would probably fall over because you would have forgotten how to stand! Except for those things that you do by instinct, such as breathing, you wouldn't know how to do anything at all.

One amazing thing about memory is that it works pretty well without you having to do anything. And we've already seen that your brain can remember enormous amounts of information. This is just as well, because in today's world we see more information than ever before. According to some researchers, a modern daily newspaper contains more information than a person living in ancient times would have come across in a lifetime! Yet our memories seem able to cope.

So how does your brain do it? In this part of the book we will look at some of the things scientists have discovered about how brains memorize. Some of the experiments for you to try are similar to those carried out by the scientists, so you can discover for yourself how the mind and memory work. Will your results match up to the experts'?

Before we get on to humans, let's take a look at …

Computers and Brains

How a Computer Works

One way to investigate how human memory works is to compare it to a computer:

First the information is **ENTERED** into a computer.

Then it has to be **STORED** somewhere.

Finally, you have to be able to **RETRIEVE** it as fast as possible.

These three steps happen in computers and in human brains. Computer memories and human memories have a lot in common. Just like human brains, a computer is able to:

• Store information

• Do a calculation

• Recognise a password

• Check a spelling

• Retrieve information stored a long time ago

However, as we will discover, brains are also different from computers in a lot of ways. But first of all ...

How Do Computers Remember?

Suppose that you have a piece of information you want to remember, such as 'Pandas live in China.' So that you can find it later, you might turn to, say, page 24 of a notepad, and write the words 'Pandas come from China.'

Saving information in a computer is a bit like keeping it in a notebook – except that computers don't save the information in words but in a language of numbers.

Every number is either a 0 or a 1. A computer will store the information 'Pandas come from China' as something like this:

0000100101011001100111010010111000101101010100110101001011111001

This number sequence is put away exactly were the computer knows to find it again, and each 1 and 0 is stored as a tiny electrical charge.

Where Do Computers Store Their Memories?

Computers store their memories in four different places:

ROM (Read Only Memory)
Some built-in computer chips have programs written on to them, which tell the computer how to run a game or load a file. These programs are permanent and you cannot get rid of them unless you take the computer apart. The ROM is something like the built-in 'memories' in the brain of a newborn baby, that tell it vital information such as how to breath and how to suck. These are the 'instincts' that do not have to be learnt.

Hard Drive and External Hard Drive
The hard drive is the part of the computer that stores all the games, programs and data that you have saved. These memories aren't lost when you turn off the computer, they are in permanent storage. As people are

using their computers more and more to store music and photos, you can also buy external hard drives to give greater memory to computers. The hard drive is similar to the cortex of the brain (this is the crinkly outer part that looks like a big walnut). It is here that scientists believe we store every piece of information we ever learn. A lot of information just sits there unused, waiting to be downloaded whenever it is needed.

CDs, DVDs and Memory Sticks

Not all of a computer's memories are stored inside it. Information can be saved onto a CD, DVD or memory stick and stored somewhere else. This is just like storing human memories in a photo album or diary.

RAM (Random Access Memory)

When you play a game on a computer, you call it up into what is called its random access memory. This part of the memory is like the computer's notepad where it can quickly store and retrieve information when it is running a programme. However, this is only temporary memory – unless you save this information on to your hard drive (your long-term memory) it is lost forever.

Your brain does something similar. It is able to hold some information for a short amount of time (e.g. a name) but unless you store that information in your long-term memory, it will disappear very quickly.

Computer facts

- Each 1 or 0 saved in a computer is called a 'bit'. 8 bits are called a 'byte'.

- The first electrical computer with a memory was built by Konrad Zuse of Germany in 1936.

- Until the 1950s, humans were still able to compete with computers in mental calculations. Even in the 1990s, the best human chess players beat the best computers at chess – but not any more!

- The world's biggest computers are getting more powerful all the time. Today, the most powerful can do more than 100,000,000,000,000 calculations per second (that's one hundred trillion). Some believe that's close to the rate at which the human brain can work.

- The amount of information that a computer can store has doubled every two years as technology has advanced. People used to talk about computers with Kilobytes of information. Then came Megabytes and Gigabytes, but now we are entering the era of Terabytes, which are one thousand times bigger than Gigabytes. A Terafying thought!'

Experiment 9 – Test Your Speed

In this experiment you will be asked four questions to which you will almost certainly know the answers. The real test is discovering how long it takes to retrieve the answers from your memory? See if you can 'feel' how long they take to answer:

Question 1: Is Germany a country?

Question 2: Is 'Rolt' an English word?

Question 3: Name a fruit that begins with the letter 'P'.

Question 4: Hum the last line of the song *Happy Birthday To You.*

How did you do? Which question took the longest to answer? Germany *is* a country. Rolt is *not* an English word. You may have thought of a pear, a peach, a pineapple, a plum or even a pomegranate. Some things can be recalled almost instantly, but others need a much longer search. To remember the last line of *Happy Birthday To You*, you probably needed to retrieve the whole song first, then sing it through from beginning to end. It is very difficult to remember the last line of a song without going through most of the other lines first!

The average time it takes to answer the questions is:

1 Under half a second
2 Just under one second
3 Just over one second
4 Two or three seconds

Every answer relied on memories stored in your brain. As you can see from the times taken, the speed at which you grab information from your memory is not always the same.

This happens with computers, too, although they are generally much faster than human brains are at retrieving information.

What Are the Differences Between a Computer and a Brain?

A computer and a brain may have a lot in common, but there are lots of differences too. One difference is that we know exactly how computer memories work because we invented them, but we still know very little about how human memories work.

Here are some other important differences between computer memories and human memories:

Computer Memory

1 Computer memories can become full – you get a scary message telling you 'Error – memory full.'

2 Computers don't forget what you put into them.

3 Computers remember things perfectly – what you give them is what they give you back. But watch out: 'GARBAGE IN, GARBAGE OUT!' is a wise old saying!

4 Computers don't decide what to remember. They just remember everything you feed into them.

5 You can expand computer memory by putting in more storage. You can even have a memory transplant.

6 Each computer memory is stored in a single place.

7 If you destroy pieces of memory chip within a computer, you can tell immediately that the computer has gone wrong.

8 Computers don't have sudden memory flashbacks when they are taken to a new place.

9 Computers find handwriting, speech and faces very hard to recognise, and they often make mistakes.

Human Memory

1 As far as we know, brains never become full, though it may feel like it after some classes!

2 Human brains do forget, especially if they aren't exercised.

3 Humans often distort their memories. Have you noticed how older people say things like: 'Children were always polite and well behaved when I was young.'

4 Human brains are selective – they remember things they think are important or which form memorable patterns.

5 To make a human memory bigger you have to make better use of what you have got. And there's no such thing as a brain transplant ... yet.

6 A single human memory may be stored in several different places in the brain.

7 If you remove small bits of brain, it is sometimes impossible to tell that anything has happened. The brain rebuilds the memories using the surviving cells.

8 Human memories can be jogged by simply walking into a room.

9 Human brains find handwriting, speech and faces very simple to remember and recognise.

So, some pretty big differences, wouldn't you say? Not being damaged when you remove pieces? Never getting full? Let's investigate the human memory a little more …

How Else Is Human Memory Different from Computer Memory?

'WHAT DO YOU CALL A BABY KANGAROO?'

A computer answers a question like this by simply looking things up methodically in its database. It's as if a little person is sent off to look through each file in order. It goes through the animal files until it finds the one marked 'kangaroo'. Then it looks in turn at each fact about kangaroos:

size …

average weight …

where found …

lifespan …

name of baby … AHA!

A BABY KANGAROO IS A JOEY.

The answer is then delivered immediately to the computer screen.

The way the brain remembers is very different. Instead of going through every brain cell in turn, it is as if a little person shouts to all the brain cells:

'HEY, DOES ANYONE KNOW ANYTHING ABOUT BABY KANGAROOS?'

At this, the brain cells go crazy! Any part of the brain that recognises any word in the question gets excited.

'I KNOW BABIES ARE YOUNG,' says one part.

'I KNOW KANGAROOS ARE FROM AUSTRALIA,' shouts another.

'I KNOW KANGAROOS HAVE POUCHES,' says a third.

This reminds other brain cells of different things.

'AUSTRALIA HAS LOTS OF DESERT,' says one (which isn't very helpful).

'KANGAROO BABIES LIVE IN POUCHES,' says another.

As soon as it hears this last message about kangaroo babies, another brain cell says:

'HEY, THE KANGAROO BABY IN THE POUCH IS A JOEY!'

At last, the right memory has been found.

This answer rockets its way back to the little person who asked the question, who sends it to the part of the brain that creates words and operates speech.

Although it doesn't really happen quite like that, you can see that the way the brain works, by firing off in many different directions at once, looks a lot less organised than a computer. The reason for this is that the brain thinks by linking together lots of different ideas.

It's as if every part of the brain asks itself, 'Now, what does that remind me of?'

Experiment 10 – Word Chain

Here is a word chain experiment to try out on yourself or with friends. Your task is to create a chain of six words. Starting with the word chosen below, write down a word that links to it. Then write down another word that links to that one and so on, until you have a chain of six words. Here is an example that starts with **WINDOW**:

WINDOW makes you think of **GLASS** (a window is made from it)

GLASS makes you think of **DRINK** (you drink from a glass)

DRINK makes you think of **COLA** (a drink)

COLA makes you think of **BUBBLES** (they fizz up in the cola)

BUBBLES makes you think of **FLOATING** (which is what bubbles do!) so the word chain goes:

WINDOW ... GLASS ... DRINK ... COLA ... BUBBLES ...
FLOATING

Now make your own six-word chain starting with **LION**

LION _____   _____   _____

_____   _____

Try this out with different people to see where the chain ends up. You should find that everybody's chain of thought is different. For example, three people who each began with **LION**, finished with **ADVERTISING**, **PIZZA**, and **SWAMP**! This shows how the same word can set off trains of thought that run in opposite directions!

Brain Scientists

In many careers, memory is an especially important part of the job. For example, an actor has to learn lines, a pilot has to remember how to operate flight controls and a nurse has to recognise a normal temperature. However, there are some jobs in which memory and the human brain play a major part.

Neuroscientists

A neuroscientist studies the brain and the way it works by performing all sorts of tests on the human nervous system. The brain is the most important part of the nervous system and there is nothing a neuroscientist enjoys more than cutting open a patient's head and examining the brain inside. Those neuroscientists who work in hospitals are known as neurologists, or brain surgeons. Neurologists have discovered all sorts of things about how memory works by examining the brains of people who have lost their memories in accidents or through illness.

Psychologists

This is pronounced 'sy-kollo-jists' (with a silent 'p', as in rasPberry). A psychologist studies people in order to understand how they think and why they behave in a certain way. Like a neurologist, a psychologist is interested in knowing how the brain works, but does this simply by observing a patient and asking questions. Psychologists do not use needles, knives and test tubes in their experiments!

Zoologists

This is pronounced 'zoo-olo-jists'. As you might guess from the word 'zoo', the job of these scientists is to study animals. They examine everything to do with animals, such as where they live, how they survive in winter and how they breed. Zoologists are also interested in discovering how animals' brains work. Many tests have been done to see how animals learn and remember. Pigs, chimpanzees, cats, dogs, rats, goldfish and even worms have been studied in experiments, with some fascinating results. Studying animals helps zoologists to understand the way the human brain works. Let's look now at some of the discoveries made so far about memory and the human brain.

How Does Your Brain Work?

Your brain is about the same size and shape as two adult fists put together. It is divided into two halves, joined together by a part called the *corpus callosum*.

Although these two halves of the brain may look identical, they have very different functions. Each half looks after one side of the body. But it is a strange fact that the LEFT half of your brain controls the RIGHT half of your body, while the RIGHT half your brain controls the LEFT half of your body. We know this because when people suffer injury, or a stroke (a burst blood vessel) to half of their brain, it is always the *opposite* half of their body that is affected.

One special part of the brain is known as the 'hippocampus'. It seems to deal with short-term memory and the memory of events that happen to you. The name originates from the Greek word *hippokampos*, meaning seahorse, because of its curved shape. We'll be seeing the hippocampus again later on in the book.

The drawing shows the parts of the brain that are important for memories and remembering.

1. The hippocampus is buried here. It is vital for short-term memory.

2. The temporal lobe. If this area is touched with an electrical probe, memories suddenly appear!

3. The left half of the brain. This controls the right half of the body, as well as language and numbers.

4. The right half of the brain. This controls the left half of the body, as well as pictures and feelings.

5. The Cerebral Cortex or 'grey matter' covers most of the brain. Memories are stored all over this area.

6. The tip of the tongue. Memories don't really appear there!

Through the work of neurologists, many things have been discovered about the brain. For one, it has no pain sensors, which means you could stay wide awake while a brain surgeon poked around inside your head – and you wouldn't feel anything!

Certain areas of the brain have very precise jobs to do. For example, there is one particular part that controls your left thumb and another in charge of your tongue. Scientists even think that there is a separate part that controls laughter. In every right-handed person, these controlling parts of the brain are usually in exactly the same places.

Brain Science Quiz

Now that you are a brain expert, test your friends with this brain-teasing quiz:

1   If you poke around inside somebody's brain with an electrical probe, which of these is most likely?

(a) The patient suddenly forgets their name.

(b) The patient says, 'You just reminded me of Batman!'

(c) The patient says, 'Ooh, that thing you're poking with is tickling me!'

(d) The patient shoots upwards and smashes through the ceiling.

2   In which of these operations might a patient forget almost nothing?

(a) Removal of little pieces of brain from several places.

(b) Removal of a big lump of brain from one place.

(c) Dropping a one ton weight on to the patient's head.

(d) Replacing the brain with a bowl of jelly.

3   What usually happens if the part that joins the two halves of the brain (the *corpus callosum*) is sliced in two?

(a) The patient pulls a horrific face and lets out a blood-curdling scream.

(b) The patient is unharmed but loses some of the coordination between the left and right sides of the body.

(c) The patient forgets everything that he has ever learnt.

(d) The patient immediately drops dead.

Answers

1 (b) Poking in the brain brings back memories. It can also make a part of the patient's body twitch uncontrollably, but not enough to send the patient through the ceiling! In the 1950s, neurologist Wilder Penfield sometimes operated on people with brain disease. As he poked around inside with an electrical probe, the patient (who was awake) might suddenly experience a forgotten childhood memory, or would jerk a hand in the air. By poking different parts of the brain, Penfield discovered that different memories link with different parts of the brain.

2 (a) A neuroscientist called Lashley (scientists are often known by just their last names) discovered that removing small pieces from different parts of the brain resulted in very little memory loss for the patient. However, removing a large chunk from one part of the brain resulted in a large amount of memory loss for the patient. Powerful electric shocks can also remove large chunks of memory.

3 (b) At one time, neurologists routinely separated the two halves of an epileptic patient's brain because they believed it would cure them of fits. Through these operations they made many interesting discoveries about the human brain. You might think that having your brain sliced down the middle would be one of the worst forms of torture. However, you wouldn't feel a thing, and could live a fairly normal life afterwards. It does sometimes happen, however, that the patient's actions are affected. For example, the left hand may want to fasten a button holding it in one way, but the right hand fights to hold it another way.

Does your brain ever get full?

An ordinary desktop computer contains about a giga-byte of storage – room for a lot of information. How-ever, one neuroscientist estimates that the capacity of the human brain is an astonishing 100,000 gigabytes! Another scientist has worked out that we are able to store about 2 bits of new information per second. Over a lifetime this means we store about 1 gigabyte. Maybe this explains why our brains never get full ...

Left- and Right-Handedness

Experiment 11 – Left or Right?

Answer the following questions:

Which hand do you prefer to write with? _____

Which foot do you prefer to kick a ball with?

_____

Which ear do you usually hold a telephone to?

_____

Which hand do you prefer to hold a tennis racket with? _____

Which hand do you prefer to throw a ball with?

_____

Which hand do you hold a knife in? _____

Most people answer 'right' to all of the above questions. Did you?

About one person in ten prefers to write with their left hand. If all your answers were 'right', see if you can find somebody who answers one of the questions with 'left'. Quite a few people who usually use their right hand hold a bat or a racket in their left hand, and some

90

hold a phone to their left ear. However, it is rare to find somebody who prefers to use their left hand for everything. This is why scientists classify people into two types, 'right-handers' and 'not-right-handers'. The 'not-right-handers' are people with different degrees of left-handedness!

Left- and right-handedness depend on how your brain is wired up. In a 'left-hander', control areas that are normally found in the left half of the brain might be in the right half. Nobody is sure why this should be the case, but one theory is that it happens in babyhood. It could be that if a baby uses the left hand the first time it picks up a toy, then the brain adapts itself to using that hand every time.

One really curious thing is that most animals do not seem to be right-handed. For example, which paw does your dog shake hands with? Which paw does your cat use if it is trying to open a cat flap? Scientists have found that about half the time they use the right paw and half the time the left paw.

Long ago, people used to think that left-handers were either stupid or evil. The word 'sinister', which means evil, is also the Latin word for 'left'. At one time, left-handed children were forced to use their right hands by having their left hands tied behind their backs! Today, our attitudes to left-handedness are different. Some people even claim that left-handers are cleverer and more creative than right-handers. There is some evidence that left-handedness is linked to good artistic skills, but it is by no means certain. What do you think?

How ticklish are you?

Scientists have been carrying out some experiments to try and find out whether people are more ticklish on their left or right sides. Of the 34 volunteers tested, 26 were more sensitive to being tickled on the right side of the body. It didn't seem to matter whether people were left or right-handed or on which side they were tickled first.

Left- and right-brain experiments

Although your memories are stored fairly evenly across the two halves of your brain, the halves work in different ways. The left and right halves of the brain don't just control the right and left sides of the body, they also have different roles. For example, words and meanings are usually stored in the left half of the brain, while tunes and pictures are mostly stored in the right. We know this from the studies made on people who have suffered brain damage. One man who had a stroke in the left half of his brain was unable to talk, but he could still sing!

In another study, a patient whose brain had been sliced down the middle, so the two halves were disconnected, was shown a picture of a banana with his right eye covered up. The patient's right-brain half recognised the banana and knew it reminded him of fruit but was unable to name it. When the right eye was uncovered, the left half of the brain went into action and remembered the name!

Here is another remarkable brain experiment to try out for yourself. It was made famous by a psychologist called Julian Jaynes.

Experiment 12 – Happy Faces!

On page 115 are two pictures of faces. DON'T LOOK YET! But when you do look:

Look straight at the nose. Look quickly at the first face, then at the second face, and decide which one you think looks happier.

NOW, QUICKLY LOOK AT EACH FACE
AND TURN BACK TO THIS PAGE.

OK, have you done it? Which face did you think was happier?

When Jaynes did this experiment, he found that about 80 per cent of right-handed people think that the face on the right is happier. Yet the two faces are identical, except that one is the mirror image of the other. Why do you think most people choose the right-hand face? If you stare at the nose, your right eye is looking mainly at the right half of the face and your left eye at the left half. The right half of the brain deals more with emotions than the left half, so what the left eye sees will influence your thinking. If your left eye sees 'sad' that's what you will think. Did it work for you?

Memory and Eye Movements

It is sometimes possible to watch a person remembering something. Have you noticed that when you are thinking, your eyes often point up or down, left or right? This may be a clue about the way that your brain is working and remembering. When your eyes move to the right this may be because your left half of the brain is busy at work.

There are some psychologists who believe that the direction in which your eyes move shows exactly what type of thought is going through your brain.

Thinking about feelings or smells

Remembering a sound

Imagining a picture

Creating a sound

Remembering a picture

Do you think that there is any truth in this theory? So far, scientists have not found much evidence to support it. Here is your chance to help out the scientists by testing it out further with this next experiment.

Experiment 13 - Watch the Eyes Move

It is very hard to test yourself for eye movements, so find a willing friend or parent to be your subject. Whoever you use must be right-handed, and remember: DON'T TELL THEM WHAT YOU ARE LOOKING FOR! You will also need an assistant to ask the questions.

Question 1: John is taller than Peter but smaller than Harry. Who is the tallest?

(To answer this question the brain needs to do some sorting. The left half of the brain usually handles this, so the eyes should point to the right.)

Question 2: Can you remember how many sides a sugar cube has?

(With this question, the subject must imagine a three-dimensional object. Visualising is thought to be handled by the right half of the brain, so the eyes should point to the left.)

Scientists carrying out this experiment have found that although the eye movements often move in the way shown, this is not always the case. What do you think?

How Long Does Memory Last?

Experiment 14 – What Is Your Earliest Memory?

What is the very earliest thing in your life that you can remember? Can you remember what your very first day at school was like? Can you remember the day your little brother or sister was born?

Try this question out on your parents and see how far back they can remember. Ask your friends too, but watch out for cheating. Some people convince themselves they can 'remember' some event from when they were a baby when, in fact, they only know about it from an old family photograph. So what was the youngest age that people can remember from?

Most people can remember very little of what happened to them before the age of five. To remember anything before the age of three is quite unusual. For many children, their earliest memory is of something exciting or scary, such as moving house, being a bridesmaid or breaking an arm!

By the way, this doesn't mean that two-year-olds have no memory. For example, most two-year-olds remember if they have been promised a treat, and are quick to remind their parent about it, but their memories don't last very long.

Even when they are older, people have some memories that are very brief. Some only last about ten seconds, which is perfectly OK as you don't need to remember everything forever. Scientists classify memory in two categories: the short-term memory and the long-term memory.

The short-term memory is like having a whiteboard in your brain. When you hear words or do a sum, it is almost as if you take a pen to write them on to your short-term board. Unfortunately, the board is quite small, so unless the information on it is transferred for storage in your long-term memory, your mind gets full and cannot take in any more.

Try this experiment to see how big your short-term whiteboard memory is.

Experiment 15 – How Many Numbers Can You Remember?

Here is a test of your short-term memory. See how many numbers you can remember in sequence. First, cover up all the numbers below and on the opposite page.

Now, uncover the first set of numbers, read it through once to yourself (not aloud), then cover it up again. Can you remember all of them? Try each set in turn.

First set   7   4   8   3   6

Did you remember all five? Now reveal the second set and see if you can remember all six digits. Keep going until you make a mistake.

Second set	2	6	5	4	9	8			
Third set		8	3	2	6	7	4	9	
Fourth set	2	7	6	3	9	8	5	6	
Fifth set		9	3	5	8	6	7	1	2	4

How far did you remember? If you got the fifth set with nine digits exactly right, you are quite unusual. Most people can remember five digits, but few can remember more than seven – the same length as a lot of phone numbers. These digits go into your short-term memory. If someone tells you a phone number, you are usually able to save it in your short-term memory for several minutes – certainly long enough to allow you to dial it!

A short-term joke ...

Patient: 'Doctor, doctor, I have this terrible problem with my short-term memory.'

Doctor: 'How long have you had this problem?'

Patient: 'What problem?'

On the other hand, some memories last for a lifetime. In 1997, Frenchwoman Jeanne Calment died aged 122. At the end of her life she was still able to remember events and experiences from the year 1885! She recorded a CD of her memories, which included the building of the Eiffel Tower in Paris in 1889 and meeting the artist Van Gogh.

Different Types of Memory

Apart from phone numbers, there are lots of different things that it is important to remember. For example:

PEOPLE'S NAMES AND OTHER FACTS ABOUT THEM

BIG EVENTS IN YOUR LIFE, SUCH AS YOUR FIRST DAY AT SCHOOL, OR THE TIME YOU FELT ILL ON A CAR TRIP

SKILLS, SUCH AS SWIMMING, RIDING A BIKE OR KICKING A BALL

You even have to remember what is in the future! Such as remembering you have to do some homework tonight. Or that your favourite TV show will be on at 8 o'clock.

These are different types of memories. We know this because when a person's brain is not working properly, it is common to hold on to some types of memories but completely lose other kinds. Do you remember the hippocampus from the 'How Does Your Brain Work' section? If it is damaged, then all sorts of weird things can happen.

One patient, known as 'Mr W', recovered from a rare brain infection which probably damaged his hippocampus. Although he was otherwise well, his memory for very recent events had disappeared. As a result he lost all sense of time. Now, if his wife leaves the room for only a few minutes and then returns, Mr W greets her as if it is the first time he has seen her in weeks. All memory of what has happened to him recently is missing. Although he can still learn new skills, he may have no memory of how he learnt them.

In another case, a man lost his short-term memory in a fencing accident. During a contest, his opponent's sword was thrust up the man's nose and into the hippocampus in his brain.

The moral of the story is:

NEVER PUT POINTED OBJECTS UP YOUR NOSE!

Forgetting

What have you forgotten in the last week? Did you forget to do homework? Did you forget somebody's name? Did you forget how to spell a familiar word?

Why do people forget? Scientists have done a lot of research into this because they know that as people get older, they seem to forget more and more often. They would like to know if it is possible to 'cure' the problem of forgetfulness.

This makes forgetting sound like a totally bad thing, which it isn't. In fact, it would be a real problem if you were unable to forget some things. If you *never* forgot, you would start to get very confused. Suppose you went shopping every week. After a while you'd have so many lists in your head that your brain would be clogged up.

Forgetting is useful because it helps you to remove all the clutter so that you can concentrate on what is really important. Forgetting is sometimes deliberate – you are able to get rid of anything you don't want to remember, such as pain or sadness.

What causes people to forget?

Although sometimes it can be good to forget, very often it can be a real nuisance! Scientists think that there are three main reasons why we forget things:

- **People forget information if they store it and never use it**
  Suppose that you learn that the French word for guinea pig is 'cobaye'. You may know this now, but it is possible that you will never need to use this information again. Eventually, the little pathway in your brain that links in to 'cobaye' slowly disappears and the memory is lost. To keep a memory you have to exercise it every so often.

- **Feeling worried or upset causes forgetfulness**
  The more you worry about how bad your memory is, the worse it becomes. One of the secrets of remembering things is to learn how to relax and not think too hard!

- **Damage to brain cells causes forgetting**
  It is a fact that too much alcohol kills brain cells. In 1994, an Australian scientist said that Australians had the world's highest incidence of memory loss because they drank so much beer! Many other mind-affecting drugs probably cause serious memory loss too, although just how much is still not really known. Sometimes the effects of taking a drug aren't known until 20 years after they have been taken.

Many women temporarily lose some of their brain-power, including memory, when they are pregnant. If you ask your mother about this, she will probably tell you that it happened to her. Scientists are not sure why this happens and the brain returns to normal within a few months of giving birth.

Another cause of temporary memory loss is a bang on the head. A cartoon character, hit on the head with a huge mallet, nearly always asks afterwards, 'Who am I?' or 'Where am I?' This can actually happen in real life, although only if the bang is very nasty and far more painful than a cartoon makes it look. A person suffering a bang on the head often forgets what happened just before the accident. In some serious cases, however, a person can forget almost everything about themselves and their past. This is a condition called 'amnesia'.

The longest lasting known case of amnesia happened to American John R. Crosswhite in 1936. He lost consciousness in a car accident and when he came to, he thought his name was John Cross. As a result of this mistake, 'John Crosswhite' was believed missing and officially declared dead in 1940. Later, John Cross got married and had another family, without knowing that he already had a wife and children. In 1973, he suffered a stroke and the change to his brain made him remember who he really was!

People often remember faces but forget names. Many years ago the famous musical conductor, Sir Thomas Beecham, was at a celebration party following one of his concerts when he saw a woman he recognised. He knew that she had a husband who had an important job, but could not remember her name or what her husband did. He politely approached her and asked how her husband was and whether he was in the same job. Imagine how he felt when she replied, 'He is very well, and yes, he is still King.'

Some very clever people can appear to have terrible memories. A friend of famous mathematical genius, David Hilbert, once showed him a complicated formula on a blackboard.

Hilbert was very impressed, and said, 'Why, that's brilliant! Who discovered that?'

'You did!' said the friend.

Hilbert did not necessarily have a bad memory. Many clever people are just absent-minded, that is, they don't pay attention because their minds are thinking about too much.

Taking memory too far

Sometimes, forcing the mind to memorize can be taken too far. American William James Sidis was the son of a Harvard University psychologist. From an early age he was trained to learn and remember. At age 7, William had completed eight years of schoolwork in six months and had mastered five languages! He went on to Harvard University, graduating with the highest honours and became a university lecturer at the age of 14. However, by 25 he was working as an ordinary book-keeper. When asked why he did this he replied, 'I am happy; this job lets me forget.'

How to prove an adult is forgetting!

Most adults believe that they are losing their memories. You can help to prove it for them with this test. The conversation will probably go something like this:

You: 'A man lived in a Bungalow. Everything inside was painted PINK. So what colour was the carpet?'

Adult: 'PINK!'

You: 'What colour was the microwave?'

Adult: 'PINK!'

You: 'What colour were his windows?'

Adult: 'PINK!'

You: 'What colour were the stairs?'

Adult: 'PINK?'

You: 'WRONG! There weren't any stairs, he lived in a bungalow. Have you forgotten already?'

THEN PREPARE TO RUN!

The Memory Can Play Tricks!

Sometimes the problem is not that we forget, but that we remember wrongly. We become convinced of a memory that turns out to be completely false. Has this ever happened to you? Let's try an experiment in recalling information.

Experiment 16 – How Accurate Is Your Recall?

Think about the clocks in your home. Only concentrate on the analogue clocks – those that have big and little hands. Perhaps there is one in your kitchen or sitting room, or maybe you have an analogue wristwatch? Close your eyes and picture the clock, then draw the face. What are the numbers like? How are the minutes marked? When you have done this, have a look at the real thing. Were you right?

It is amazing how often people get this wrong, even though they look at these clocks every single day. This test was tried out on a class of eight-year-olds who had a big clock in their classroom. The clock was covered up and they tried drawing it. All but one of them drew a clock something like this:

One of the children knew this was wrong, and he drew this:

However, when the clock was uncovered, it looked like this:

It had no numbers all, not even Roman numerals. Everyone had convinced themselves that they had 'remembered', but their memories were wrong!

Accurate memory recall is particularly important in a law court. Most cases rely on witnesses telling the judge what they remember. Even if people are telling what they believe is the truth, their memories can sometimes fool them. In an experiment a psychologist asked a room full of people to watch a film showing a car running into a lamppost. The people were then split into two groups. One group was asked:

'How fast do you think the car was going when it HIT the lamppost?'

The second group was asked:

'How fast do you think the car going when it SMASHED INTO the lamp post?'

The slightly different wording in these two questions shouldn't have made any difference to the answers because everyone saw the same film, but in fact it did! The first group estimated the car was being driven at about 20 miles per hour but the second group thought it was going much faster. This shows that simply by altering one word in the question, the second group's memory had been changed.

A week later, the same groups were asked if they had noticed any broken glass at the scene of the accident. The group who had heard that the car had 'smashed' into the lamppost said that there was broken glass on the road. Yet the film showed no sign of any glass. It was a false memory.

Animals and Memory

Neurologists and psychologists aren't the only people who have made discoveries about how memory works. We have also found out a great deal thanks to zoologists.

For a long time, zoologists have been interested in the idea that all animals have the ability to learn and remember. Evidence suggests that even the simplest creatures have some kind of memory. As well as learning about animals' brains, the studies scientists have carried out have helped them to learn more about the ways in which humans think and remember.

How Long Is an Animal's Memory?

In an experiment on a goldfish, researchers always left food for it in a particular part of the tank. The fish was then taken out of its own, familiar tank and put into another for short periods. The researchers found that if the goldfish was kept away from the food tank for more than ten seconds, it didn't know where to look for its food – it had 'forgotten'.

Some people say that this proves a goldfish's memory only lasts for ten seconds. This means that if you put a goldfish in a big tank, it will never get bored. By the time it has swum around the tank and arrived back to where it started, it will think it is seeing it for the first time!

This popular goldfish story is fun, but the general conclusion is probably wrong. There is lots of evidence that some species of fish can remember and learn. For centuries in China, pet carp have responded to the sound of a food bell. And any fisherman will know that if he goes to the same part of a river every day and throws bait into it, the fish will eventually start to gather in that particular spot.

Usually, the bigger an animal's brain, the better its memory. In one experiment, baboons watched where a piece of apple was hidden outside their cage and remembered where it was for up to an hour.

Have you ever heard the saying 'Elephants never forget'? Well, it isn't true! However, some people believe that elephants do have extremely good memories, especially of their owners. In 1830, an elephant keeper called Baptist Bernhard was attacked and crushed by one of his elephants. At the inquest into his death, the judge decided that the elephant was taking revenge for some cruel treatment by the keeper two years before.

Finding the Way

Pigeons have the remarkable ability to remember their way, even if they are a great distance from home. For over a thousand years carrier pigeons have been used to deliver messages, especially in times of war. In 1940 a British pigeon called Lucky Lass was parachuted into occupied France with her secret agent. After travelling some way on foot, the agent and the pigeon went into hiding while they waited for the delivery of top-secret information. After 11 days without seeing daylight, Lucky Lass was safely released with the message and flew 285 miles (480 kilometres) straight back to her pigeon loft in England.

Many species of birds, animals, fish and even insects regularly migrate on long, hazardous journeys covering hundreds, even thousands, of miles. Scientists do not yet fully understand how pigeons and other creatures find their way. One theory is that they have magnets in their brains which are sensitive to the magnetic field of the Earth and help them to navigate. Another theory is that a pigeon remembers landmarks near its home, such as a windmill or tall tree.

Amazing memories?

One cat called Toby moved house with his family. They went from Cornwall in the west of England to Kent in the south-east, going by train via London. The day after arriving at his new house, Toby decided he preferred the old home. He set off for Cornwall and, four months later, arrived back at his old house, having covered a distance of 280 miles (450 kilometres)!

But that's nothing compared with an American cat called Tommy who walked over 950 miles (1600 kilometres) from Oklahoma to his old home in California. It took 18 months and included crossing two deserts! Scientists have yet to discover whether this incredible homing instinct in certain animals is due to memory, or some other amazing ability.

Experiments

A zoologist who was interested in the idea that memory could be passed on from one animal to another carried out a gruesome experiment on flatworms. Although flatworms are simple animals with tiny brains, the scientist found that they could be taught to move towards a light to find food. When a group of flatworms had learnt to do this, he killed them and fed them to a second group. To the scientist's surprise, the second set of flatworms seemed to know immediately that they should go to the light for food. Did this mean that it is possible to learn by 'eating the memories' of other animals? The scientist thought so. However, no other scientists have been able to reproduce this experiment and get the same results. What do you think?

Experiments with chicks showed that they remembered a horrible taste after just one or two pecks at food. The ability to recognize that an unpleasant taste means something is harmful is very important. The Russian scientist, Pavlov, used dogs for one of the most famous animal experiments. Every time he fed his dogs he rang a bell. After a while, the dogs began to connect the sound of a bell with mealtime. Before long, Pavlov had only to ring the bell and the dogs would slobber as if a dish of food were in front of them.

NOW, QUICKLY LOOK AT EACH FACE BEFORE TURNING BACK TO PAGE 93

What Next?

Do you think it will ever be possible to take a person's brain and read all the memories it contains? Will somebody ever invent a formula that turns us all into memory masters? How exactly does the brain store that memory of your Aunt Suzie – as a special molecule with its own chemical formula, or as a tiny picture etched into your brain? Nobody knows – there is still a lot that we do not understand about memory.

Finding the answer to questions like these needn't be left to scientists. You have already begun investigating memory by doing the experiments in this book. So why not carry on experimenting to see what else you find out about your own and your friends' memories?

For example, you could test how long memories last. Learn a list of ten items (they could be countries, famous people, cars, TV shows) before you go to bed and see how many you can remember in the morning – then test yourself again a week later. Make a list of the kind of things you remember best and what you always seem to forget. Think up other experiments and involve friends, family, and even pets in your investigations (only if they want to!).

You can train your memory to do some great tricks that will entertain and amaze your friends, and help you to do better in exams. You can also use it to make more of the world around you. If you remember details about new people you meet, the next time you see them you will have plenty to talk about. A good memory will make an exciting trip or special occasion more fun too – the more you can remember, the clearer your memories will be.

Whatever you decide to use it for, NEVER FORGET that you have an amazing memory machine up there in your brain, just waiting to get some exercise. Why not start right now?

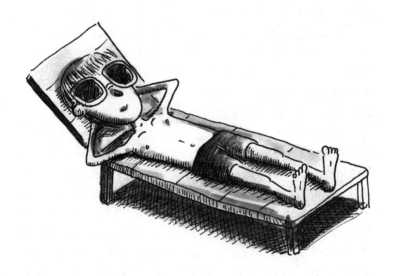

PART THREE

What Is a Mnemonic?

As we have seen in Part One of this book, a mnemonic (say 'nee-monics') is a rhyme, saying or special trick that helps you to remember useful facts or information. Mnemonic is the only word in the dictionary that begins with 'mn'. It is named after Mnemosyne (Nem-o-sine), the ancient Greek goddess of memory.

People use mnemonics for all kind of things, from helping to tie their shoelaces, to remembering difficult spellings, recalling famous dates or learning the names of countries. Everyone needs a mnemonic at some time!

The best mnemonics are those that are easy to learn. Good mnemonics usually rhyme or have a rhythmic pattern or, best of all, make you laugh. Complicated or boring mnemonics have been left out of this collection.

You'll be surprised at how quickly you will learn all the mnemonics. When you've done so why not try making up some of your own? Those that you make up yourself are usually the most memorable of all.

This section is a collection of the mnemonics I like best, ones that I find really useful and that I hope you will have great fun learning.

50 Fantastic Mnemonics

1 Left and Right

Many people have problems remembering which is their left and which is their right hand. Many adults have to remind themselves sometimes!

Here is the best way to teach somebody their left hand from their right hand. Hold your hands in front of you like this:

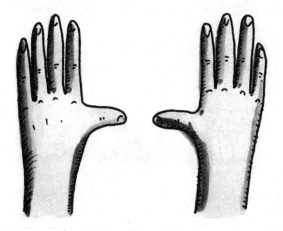

Your LEFT hand makes a better L shape, so that is how to tell which hand is left.

2 North South East and West

Once you know left from right, you should learn east from west. This is how the directions look on a compass:

One way to help remember the order is that WE spells a word (EW isn't a word).

Some people remember the compass by starting at the top and moving around it clockwise, saying:

Never Eat Sour Watermelons

Or

Naughty Elephants Squirt Water.

Have you ever noticed, by the way, that NESW stands for:

Nowhere, Everywhere, Somewhere and Where.

They are all the 'where' words – a curious coincidence.

3 Reading a Map

You are in a submarine and in front of you is a map. The radar operator tells you that he has picked up a battleship in the square with the co-ordinates 2,4. Which position is the battleship? Is it X or Y?

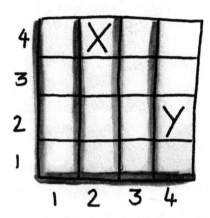

To remember how to read co-ordinates, think about what happens when you walk into a house. You go:

Along the hallway and up the stairs.

When you read map co-ordinates, first go along the hallway, and then up the stairs! The battleship is 2 along the bottom and 4 up. So it is at X. This works for reading any kind of map.

4 Port and Starboard

On a ship, the left and right sides of the boat are known as port and starboard – but which is which? People often get confused but the easiest rule of memory is this one:

PORT is LEFT and both words have FOUR letters.

STARBOARD is RIGHT and both words are longer.

The light on the port side of a boat is red and on the starboard side is green. You can remember this because red is also the colour of a strong wine called port. When port wine is drunk after a meal the tradition is to fill your glass and then

Pass the port bottle to your left (your port side!).

5 Which way to turn ...

Here are two simple ways to remember how to tighten or loosen a valve or a screw.

**Righty tighty,
Lefty loosie.**

**Turn it right (clockwise)
To make it tight!**

You also turn to the right (clockwise) when you are locking a door with a key.

6 Sunset

One important way of knowing which direction you are going is by knowing where the sun rises and where it sets. How can you remember that the sun rises in the east and sets in the west?

E stands for EARLY and EAST.

Japan is known as the 'Land of the Rising Sun' and it is in the east.

You can work out the directions at lunchtime because at noon in the northern hemisphere the sun is in the south.

7 Changing the Clocks

Most countries shift their clocks by an hour twice during the year so they can make the most of the daylight. The rule for remembering which way the clocks move in spring and fall (autumn) is this:

Spring FORWARD,

Fall BACK.

Clocks are put forward one hour in spring and back one hour in fall.

8 Months of the Year

How many days are there in each month of the year? There is an old poem to help you to remember:

> **Thirty days has September**
> **April, June and November.**
> **All the rest have thirty-one**
> **Excepting February alone**
> **Which has twenty-eight days clear**
> **And twenty-nine in each leap year.**

Some people find this too complicated, so they say:

> **Thirty days has September**
> **All the rest I can't remember!**

The best trick is one that uses your knuckles. Hold your hands like this:

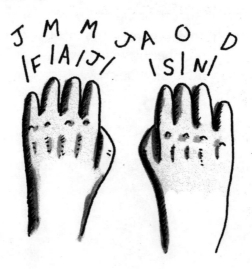

Count along your knuckles as shown. If a month is on a knuckle it has 31 days. If it is in a dip, it has 30 days (except February of course). Don't count the valley between your two hands!

9 The Moon

The moon appears and disappears in cycles of 28 days. It grows from nothing to a full moon (called waxing) and then slowly disappears back to nothing (called waning). But when you look up at it in the sky, how can you tell if the moon is waxing or waning?

In the northern hemisphere, if you can see the left-hand side of the moon (which looks like a C), the moon is WANING.

Remember this because:

C is for 'C ya later', or 'Ciao'.

If you can see the right-hand side (a 'D'), the moon is WAXING.

Remember this because:

D is for 'Developing'.

10 Planets

Which is nearer to Earth? Saturn or Jupiter? Mercury or Venus? Here are the planets in order:

M V E M J S U N P

Mercury Venus Earth Mars Jupiter Saturn Uranus Neptune Pluto

These two simple phrases will help you to remember the order of the planets going away from the sun:

> **My Very Easy Method Just Speeds Up Naming Planets.**
>
> **My Very Eager Mother Just Served Us Nine Pizzas.**

This is usually the order of the planets. However, because their orbits are different shapes, Pluto is sometimes closer to the sun than Neptune. By the way, astronomers now think Pluto isn't a planet after all. Spoilsports!

Also, have you noticed that the initials of:

> **Saturn Uranus Neptune**
> spell **SUN** ?

11 Weather Forecasting

Farmers and others who work in the open air have always found it useful to have little aids to help them to forecast the weather. One famous saying is:

> **Red sky at night,**
> **Shepherd's delight.**
> **Red sky at morning,**
> **Shepherd's warning.**

You may have also heard it as 'sailor's delight'. A red sky at night and a beautiful sunset usually means that there is high pressure in the atmosphere, which means you can expect good, clear weather.

Another true saying goes:

> **If the stars shine bright,**
> **It will be a cold night.**

That is because clear skies mean that there are no clouds to give the Earth a blanket.

This is a saying for people who love good weather:

> **When the dew is on the grass, rain will**
> **never come to pass.**

Animals often sense the weather before we do. So watch out ...

> **If the cows are lying down,**
> **Rain will soon be on the ground.**
> **When birds fly from sea to land,**
> **A raging storm is soon at hand.**

12 Rainbows

Rainbows appear when the sun is shining and it is raining at the same time. The rainbow appears on the opposite side to you from the sun. The water droplets in the air split the sunlight into a spectrum, which is why we see all the different colours. The scientist Isaac Newton listed the colours in 1704. Some say he could only see five – red, yellow, green, blue, and violet – but his assistant had better eyesight and added orange and indigo. The colours of the rainbow, starting at the top are:

Red Orange Yellow Green Blue Indigo Violet

One way to remember them is by saying:

Richard Of York Gave Battle In Vain.

(Richard of York was the English king, Richard III, who lost in battle against Henry VII.)

Another way to remember the order is to imagine a man named:

ROY G. BIV

13 The Western United States

There are 50 states in the USA and there are many methods for learning them. Here is a way of remembering the states in one area:

Just remember the word:

WONC!

It stands for the four western states:

Washington
Oregon
Nevada
California

But be careful – NEVada NEVer touches the sea!

14 The Mississippi

The longest river in the USA is the Mississippi. How do you spell Mississippi? Put in as many Is, Ss and Ps as you can and you won't go too far wrong! The five states that run down the left-hand side of the Mississippi spell:

MIMAL

Minnesota Iowa Missouri Arkansas and Louisiana

There is also a rhyme that goes:

**M-I-S
S-I-S
S-I-P-P-I
It used to be
So hard to spell
It used to make me cry!**

15 World's Seven Longest Rivers

Which are the world's longest rivers? Most books agree on the top seven, but none of them agree on the order. It all depends on how you measure the length. Anyway, you won't be far wrong if you remember them in this order:

NILE (mainly in Egypt)

AMAZON (mainly in Brazil)

MISSISSIPPI (in the USA)

YANGTZE (in China)

YENISEY (in Russia)

YELLOW (in China)

OB (in Russia)

The initial letters, from last to first, are: O YYY MAN. Remember this as:

Oh Three Wise Man.

16 The Great Lakes

There are five Great Lakes in the USA. To remember the five lakes, think of the word:

HOMES

The letters stand for:

Huron

Ontario

Michigan

Erie

Superior

Lake Superior IS superior. It is the biggest of the Great Lakes and the one that is farthest north.

17 Weights and Measures

Do you ever need to convert weights and measures into metric? It can be very confusing. These helpful rhymes were made up by a cereal company to help people:

A metre measures three foot three,
It's longer than a yard, you see.

A litre of water's
A pint and three-quarters.

Two-and-a-quarter pounds of jam
Weigh about a kilogram.

18 Yards in a Mile

Here's a way to remember two things with one mnemonic:

George the Third
Said with a smile
'Seventeen sixty
Yards in a mile.'

1760 was also the year when George III became King of Britain (and the American colonies too!). Sixteen years later, during his reign, America gained independence. King George is best remembered for going 'mad' when he was old.

19 Temperature

How can you translate Fahrenheit temperatures into Centigrade? The complicated way is to subtract 32, multiply by 5 and divide by 9. However, for most temperatures on a weather chart, there is a simple rule that gets you close enough to the right answer:

Fahrenheit to Centigrade:
Take away 30 and halve it.

Centigrade to Fahrenheit:
Double and add 30.

For 10° Centigrade and 50° Fahrenheit, this formula works out exactly right!

20 Stalagmites and Stalactites

StalaCtites hang from the Ceiling
StalaGmites come up from the Ground.

Some people learn a different rule – they say:

MITES crawl up and TIGHTS fall down.

Another one goes:

StalacTITES have to hold on TIGHT or they will fall off!

21 What to Do if You Are Stung

The mild poisons in bee stings and wasp stings contain different chemicals. The rule for what to put on them is:

Bicarbonate for a Bee
Vinegar for Vasps!

22 Sports Injuries – Strains, Twists and Knocks

If you twist an ankle or break a finger, there is a rule for treating it that sports trainers use. They use the word:

RICE (or sometimes RICED)

R for Rest (sit down, don't run around)

I for Ice (put ice on the injury)

C for Compression (put on a bandage)

E for Elevation (raise the injured part above the rest of the body)

D for Doctor (call an expert)

So, next time you hear somebody shout 'RICED!' you will know what they mean!

23 Where to Get Your Vitamins

A balanced diet should include the four most important vitamins. They can be found in these foods:

Vitamin A from:
'Addock

Haddock, and any other fish, is full of Vitamin A. So are carrots!

Vitamin B from:
Brown Bread and Butter

Vitamins C from:
Citrus fruit

Vitamin D from:
Daylight

There's also a Vitamin E, but:

Vitamin E is Easy to find in nearly Every food.

24 Apples and Pears

If you plant fruit trees in the garden, you will be lucky to have fruit growing on them in the first summer. Sometimes, it takes years for fruit to start appearing on a tree. Apples start to appear when the tree is quite young, but pears don't grow on pear trees for several years. There is an old saying:

Grow apples for yourself
And pears for your heirs.

There is also a saying for corn, grown in many US states:

Knee high by the fourth of July!

25 Bird Songs

Bird watchers have all sorts of methods for identifying birds, but one of the best ways is to listen to their songs. These songs have been turned into little phrases so that the song patterns are easier to remember. Here are three:

The American Robin:
'Cheer-up, cheer-a-lee, cheer-ee-o'

The European Yellowhammer:
'A little bit of bread and no cheese'

The Mourning Dove:
'Hooh-ah hoo-hoo-hoo'

26 Know Your Camels

The camel has a single hump.
The dromedary, two,
Or else the other way around.
I'm never sure. Are you?

That rhyme was by Ogden Nash. Here is a helpful way to answer his question:

There are two common types of camel, the Bactrian and the Dromedary. If you flip the first letter of each name on its side you can see how many humps there are!

27 Know Your Elephants

The way to tell the difference between an African elephant and Indian elephant is that:

Africans have lArge ears
Indians have lIttle ears.

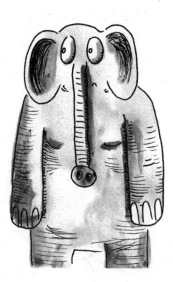

28 And Know Your Dinosaurs!

There were three prehistoric periods in which dinosaurs lived:

Triassic

Jurassic

Cretaceous

You can remember the order with this simple mnemonic:

Tyrannosaurus Jaws Crunch

29 Henry VIII, England's Most Famous King

Henry VIII was a famous king for many reasons, but he is probably remembered best because he had six wives. He divorced two of them, another died, two had their heads chopped off on his orders and one survived him.

The order of the wives was:

Catherine of Aragon

Anne Boleyn

Jane Seymour

Anne of Cleves

Catherine Howard

Katherine Parr

This is the rhyme that tells you what happened to them, in order:

Divorced, Beheaded, Died
Divorced, Beheaded, Survived!

One way to remember that Catherine Parr had the happiest end is the rhyme:

Katherine Parr
Went far!

30 Pecking Order

The most important titles in the British aristocracy are King, Queen, Prince and Princess. After that, the pecking order for men goes:

Duke

Marquis

Earl

Viscount

Baronet

Here is the way to remember it:

Dear Me, Even Viscounts Burp!

31 Kings and Queens of England

This is the most difficult mnemonic in the book, but if you want to learn British history, it is one of the best mnemonics ever invented. If you spend a bit of time learning the complete verse (which isn't that difficult), then you will know the order of every King and Queen since 1066. At the back of the book are the full names and some notes explaining the poem:

Willy, Willy, Harry, Steve
Harry, Dick, John, Harry 3
One, two, three Neds, Richard 2
Henry 4, 5, 6 then who?

Edward, Edward, Dick the Bad
Henry, Henry, Ned the Lad
Mary, Elizabeth, James the Vain
Charlie, Charlie, James again

William and Mary, Anne-a-Gloria
Four Georges, William and Victoria
Edward, George
Edward, George again

Then Elizabeth 2 began her long reign.

32 American Presidents

Here is a way to remember the first seven US presidents, who were:

Washington

Adams

Jefferson

Madison

Monroe

Adams

Jackson

You can remember this with:

**Washington And Jefferson
Made Many A Joke.**

33 Columbus

One of the most important dates in world history is the year Christopher Columbus crossed the Atlantic and discovered the West Indies off the American coast. The following year he returned on a quest for gold.

In fourteen hundred and ninety-two,
Columbus sailed the ocean blue.
In fourteen hundred and ninety-three,
Columbus stole all he could see!

34 London's Greatest Disasters

The Great Plague (otherwise known as bubonic plague) killed about 100,000 people in London in 1665. The following year, most of the city was burned down after a fire started above a baker's shop in the city.

In 1665,
The Plague left few alive.

In 1666,
London burned like sticks.

35 The Moon Landings

The men on the first moon landing were A B C ...
Armstrong, **B**uzz (Aldrin) and **C**ollins. A and B stepped
on the moon in that order, C never stepped on the
moon. They travelled on Apollo 11, which you can
write as Apo**ll**o.

36 Great Roman Leaders

The first great leader of the Roman Empire was Julius
Caesar. You can remember all of the early leaders with
this silly phrase:

Join My Aunt at The Cat Club Now!

Julius Caesar	**Caligula**
Mark Anthony	**Claudius**
Augustus	**Nero**
Tiberius	

37 Roman Numbers

The Romans used letters to represent their numbers and we still sometimes use Roman numerals today:

$$I = 1$$
$$V = 5$$
$$X = 10$$
$$L = 50$$
$$C = 100$$
$$D = 500$$
$$M = 1000$$

Remember the order with this sentence:

It's Very X-citing! Lucky Cats Drink Milk.

If you get confused between the Roman four (IV) and the Roman six (VI) then remember:

What comes after three?
The Romans say I–V.

38 Music Notes

When you read music, the higher notes appear on the treble clef part. The way to remember the notes that are written between the lines is:

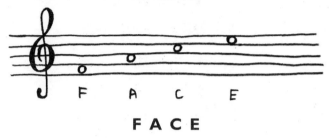

F A C E

The way to remember the notes on the lines is:

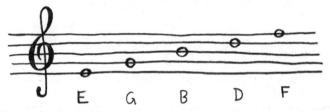

E(very) G(ood) B(oy) D(eserves) F(ootball).

It doesn't have to be football. It can be fruit or flapjacks or fish!

In the bass part, the gaps between the lines are:

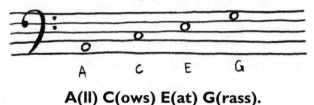

A(ll) C(ows) E(at) G(rass).

And the lines are:

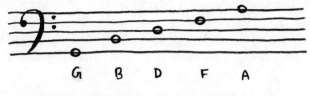

G B D F A

G(reat) B(ig) D(inners) F(or) A(ll).

39 Bach and Handel

J.S. Bach (say 'bark'!) and G.F. Handel were two great 17th-century composers. Their music is world-famous and is often still played at weddings and concerts. This little rhyme will help you to remember when they lived:

> **Bach and Handel as you know,**
> **Died and were buried long ago.**
> **Born in the year One Six Eight Five,**
> **Still they are very much alive!**

40 Monet and Manet

Claude Monet and Edouard Manet were two famous 19th- century French painters. Today, their paintings are worth a fortune. It is very easy to get them con-fused because their surnames are so alike. One helpful way to remember the difference is this:

A picture by MANet, is more
Likely to have a MAN in it.

Most of Manet's famous paintings have people as their subject – and very often one of the main figures in the pictures is a man.

Monet's paintings are more often of gardens or the countryside. He painted women and children but it is very rare to see a man as the main character.

41 I Before E

A very famous spelling aid is:

> **I before E**
> **Except after C**
> **Or when sounding like 'A'**
> **As in 'neighbour' and 'weigh'.**

For example:

> **flEld, chIEf, achIEve, pIEce**

but:

> **recEIve, cEIling, concEIt**

Unfortunately, this doesn't always work. Here are some common exceptions:

> **THEIR and LEISURE don't belong to the rule.**
> **WEIRD is a weird spelling and so is SEIZE.**

42 Stationary and Stationery

These two words are easy to get confused. One means paper, envelopes and other office equipment. The other means not moving. The way to tell which is which is to remember that:

Envelopes are a type of stationEry

When they are pARked, cARs are stationARy.

43 Other Assorted Spellings

So many words have mnemonics to help you to spell them that there isn't space to include them all here. You can probably invent some for yourself. Here are four examples that should stick in you mind:

A friEND is always there in the END.

Question: 'Do you eat DESERT or DESSERT?'

Answer: 'You eat DeSSert because you get twice as much!'

BECAUSE:

Big Elephants Can Always Understand Small Elephants.

And finally to spell:

NECESSARY:

Never Eat Crabs, Eat Salmon Sandwiches And Remain Young.

That last mnemonic is so long that it would probably have been easier to remember the word! However, I still whisper this sentence to myself as I am spelling 'necessary!'

44 Yours Sincerely

If you start a letter with:

'Dear Sir or Madam'

You must finish it with:

'Yours faithfully'

If you address a letter to:

'Mr, Mrs or Dr'

You must end with:

'Yours sincerely'

The rule is that two S's never go together:

SIR never goes with SINCERELY

45 Nine Times Table

To work out your nine times table, hold your hands like this:

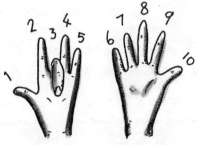

1 2 3 4 5 6 7 8 9 10

To multiply 9 by 3, fold down the third finger and then count the number of fingers to the left and right of it. There are:

2 fingers on the left and 7 on the right

so 3 times 9 is 27!

This works for all the fingers, so 6 times 9 is:

5 (left) and 4 (right) or 54

46 Remembering Pi

The distance around a circle is called the circumference. The radius is the length from the centre to the edge. The formula for working out what the circumference measures is:

pi x the radius x 2

But what is pi? It's slightly more than 3 but cannot be written down because it goes on forever! This mnemonic will help you to remember the first 8 digits which are 3.1415926. Count the number of letters in each word:

May I have a large container of coffee?

3   1   4   1   5   9   2   6

One Japanese man learnt 42,000 digits of pi by heart, but I don't know of a simple mnemonic for it!

47 Two Tricky Square Roots

Everyone knows that 2 is the square root of 4 because 2 x 2 = 4. The square root of 2 is approximately 1.414. To remember it say:

The root of 2?
I WISH I KNEW.

Then count up the letters in each word of

'I wish I knew'.

If you want to remember the square root of 3:

The root of 3?
O, SOMEONE AID ME.

Count the letters in

'O, someone aid me'

to come up with 1.732

48 Chemistry – The Smallest Atoms

If you learn chemistry, you may need to remember the nine smallest chemical atoms, which are:

Hydrogen   **Carbon**
Helium   **Nitrogen**
Lithium   **Oxygen**
Beryllium   **Fluorine**
Boron

To help you to remember them all, think of:

Hippity Hop! Little Benjamin Bunny Can Never Overtake Flopsy.

49 Tennis

The four most important tennis tournaments in the world are the Australian Open, the French Open, Wimbledon (in the UK) and the US Open. If a tennis player wins all four of these tournaments, he or she achieves what is called the 'grand slam'. Here is a verse that will remind you of the four major tournaments in order through the year:

S tart off the year in Australia.
L eave for France where there is tennis in May.
A dvance next to Wimbledon's straw-berries and cream
M ake the slam in the US of A.

50 The World Cup – Football

The winners of the World Cup, the most important international tournament for football, between 1970 and 1994 fitted a very neat arrangement:

1970	**Brazil**
1974	**Germany**
1978	**Argentina**
1982	**Italy**
1986	**Argentina**
1990	**Germany**
1994	**Brazil**

England won in 1966 and France in 1998 which spoils an otherwise perfect pattern!

Create Your Own Mnemonics

Now that you have read all of the mnemonics in this book, why not invent some yourself? There are hundreds of subjects for which nobody has yet thought up a really good memory aid! I don't think I have ever heard any for mountain ranges, pop singers, movie stars, capital cities, football teams … and plenty more besides. Who knows, it could be your mnemonic that everyone will use.

Order of the Kings and Queens of England

William I
Or 'Willy' for short!

William II

Henry I
Harry is another name for Henry

Steven

Henry II

Richard I
Dick is a short name for Richard

John
King John signed the Magna Carta

Henry III

Edward I
Ned is a short name for Edward

Edward II

Edward III

Richard II

Henry IV

Henry V

Henry VI
During Henry's reign, the War of the Roses began.
Different nobles were fighting to win the English crown.
This is why it says 'then who?' in the rhyme.

Edward IV

Edward V

Richard III
Richard III is known as 'Dick the Bad' because some say
that he murdered the Princes in the Tower, the sons of
Edward V.

Henry VII

Henry VIII
England's most famous king, thanks to his six wives!

Edward VI
'Ned the Lad', son of Henry VIII, was only ten years old
when he became king.

Mary

Elizabeth I

James I
James I was a vain man.

Charles I
Charles I was beheaded and England became a republic
for about ten years under Oliver Cromwell. However,
the monarchy was restored under Charles II.

Charles II

James II

William & Mary
William III and his wife Mary were joint king and queen.

Anne
'Gloria' means 'glory'.

George I

George II

George III
This George was king when America gained its independence.

George IV

William IV

Victoria

Edward VII

George V

Edward VIII
Edward gave up being king to marry a divorced woman (which was forbidden).

George VI

Elizabeth II

Darkness Visible: Inside the World of Philip Pullman

Nicholas Tucker

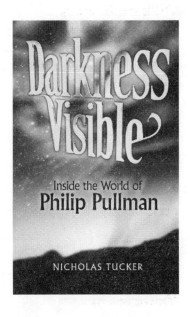

Philip Pullman is one of the world's most popular and original authors, read by children and adults alike. Containing an astonishing cast of characters, from scholarly Oxford dons to armoured bears, witches, angels, murderous Spectres and hideous harpies drawn straight from Greek mythology, Pullman's fiction can be read at many different levels.

Darkness Visible looks at the world of Philip Pullman, from the flamboyant *Sally Lockhart* series and the award winning *Clockwork* and *I Was a Rat!*, to the epic *His Dark Materials* trilogy. It shows the diverse influences – from Milton and Blake to comic books and radio drama – that have shaped his writing and uncovers the part played by Pullman's unconventional childhood.

Written by acclaimed critic Nicholas Tucker, and packed with never-before-seen family photos, illustrations from Pullman's beloved graphic novels and fresh material from recent interviews, this is both a celebration of Philip Pullman and a useful guide to the rich world of his fiction.

UK £6.99 • Canada $15.00 • ISBN 1 84046 482 8

Collections of classic poetry and prose

Edited by Kate Agnew

Wizard's collections of classic poetry and prose, introduced by some of the best-loved authors for young people, are a rollercoaster ride of emotions and experience, expressed in some of the most passionate words ever written.

'Books to curl up with ... these are substantial anthologies and the choice is rich indeed. Endlessly refreshing and intriguing ... there's never a dull moment.' *Guardian*

'Wonderful ... dispels preconceptions and encourages new audiences' *Booktrusted*

'At a time when jaunty modern verse proliferates, it's good to have such well-chosen collections of poems on the most exciting subject areas of all.' Adèle Geras, *Armadillo*

'The selection and arrangement of material is brilliant, creating cross-currents, complications, and time travelling coincidences.' *Times Educational Supplement*

All royalties from these books will go to the charity National Children's Homes

the children's charity

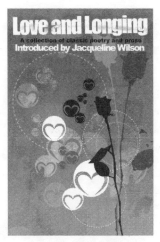

Introduced by
Jacqueline Wilson
ISBN 1 84046 523 9

Introduced by
Kevin Crossley-Holland
ISBN 1 84046 526 3

Introduced by
Philip Pullman
ISBN 1 84046 567 0

Introduced by
Michael Morpurgo
ISBN 1 84046 570 0

UK £5.99 • Canada $12.00

Dear Mr Morpingo: Inside the World of Michael Morpurgo

Geoff Fox

Dr Mr Morpingo

*I have just read your book
The Wreck of the Zanzibar.
It's the best book I have ever
read. It is miles better than
any Harry Potter book. BUT,
there's one thing definitely
wrong with this book. It's
about a girl. Write me a book
about a boy who gets stuck
on a desert island.*

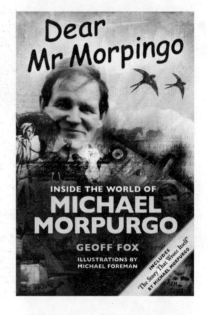

Michael Morpurgo may be
the Children's Laureate, but
readers often have trouble
spelling his name correctly. Yet thousands and thousands of
them have no trouble at all reading stories like *The Butterfly
Lion, Cool!* or *Private Peaceful*. Or *Kensuke's Kingdom*, the best-
selling story Michael wrote about a boy stranded on a desert
island to please his fan.

Dear Mr Morpingo takes you inside the world of Michael
Morpurgo to answer the questions readers love to ask –
about Michael's life, the ideas behind his stories and how
he writes.

UK £5.99 • Canada $12.00 • ISBN 1 84046 607 3

Big Numbers: A mind-expanding trip to infinity and back

Mary and John Gribbin
Illustrated by
*Ralph Edney and
Nicholas Halliday*

How big is infinity? How small is an electron?

When will the Sun destroy the Earth?

How fast is a nerve impulse in your brain?

Why can't you see inside a black hole?

What's the hottest temperature ever recorded on Earth?

What's the furthest you can see on a clear night?

Welcome to the amazing world of 'Big Numbers', where you'll travel from the furthest reaches of the known Universe to the tiniest particles that make up life on Earth. Together with Mary and John Gribbin, you can find out how our telescopes can see 10 billion years into the past, and why a thimbleful of a neutron star would contain as much mass as all the people on Earth put together!

UK £4.99 • Canada $10.00 • ISBN 1 84046 661 8

Junior Su Doku

Su Doku puzzles are great fun, challenging and very addictive.

Beginning with a comprehensive how to play section, *Junior Su Doku*, the first Su Doku book published for children, contains over 120 puzzles using numbers, letters and shapes. The book opens with some very easy 4 x 4 grids before gently increasing in difficulty to the more complex 6 x 6 and finally to the well known 9 x 9 puzzles.

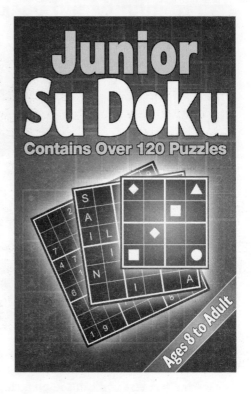

UK £3.99 • ISBN 1 84046 723 1

Kidoku

Over 200 new puzzles to enjoy in five different ways – including the brand new game sensation, Spidoku!

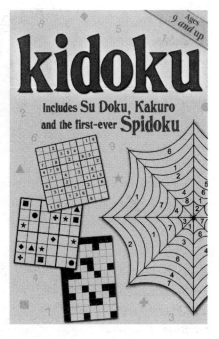

Kidoku is the ultimate children's puzzle book - the only place where you can play the world's first-ever Spidoku games alongside the classic Su Doku and the latest craze, Kakuro. Using not only numbers, but also letters and shapes, *Kidoku* contains a variety of highly addictive, pleasantly challenging, and extremely fun puzzle games.

Includes a comprehensive 'How to Play' section at the back of the book, providing invaluable hints and logic tips.

UK £3.99 • Canada $10.00 • ISBN 1 84046 750 9

The Forgotten Spell

Dare to open this book and you will be entering the strange and dangerous world of the Fey – malevolent creatures that inhabit a realm just out of reach of mortals. Few know how to find it and fewer still can return.

YOUR Quest is to search for the Forgotten Spell, long ago destroyed by the hand that first devised it – the powerful warlock, Olcrada. Here you must be prepared to test your courage, strength and wit as you journey through the cursed city of Suidemor. Can you survive?

UK £5.99 • Canada $12.00 • ISBN 1 84046 731 2

Fighting Fantasy by Wizard Books

The Warlock of Firetop Mountain
Steve Jackson and Ian Livingstone

Deep in the caverns beneath Firetop Mountain lies an untold wealth of treasure, guarded by a powerful Warlock – or so the rumour goes. Several adventurers like yourself have set off for Firetop Mountain in search of the Warlock's hoard. None has ever returned. Do you dare follow them?

Your quest is to find the Warlock's treasure, hidden deep within a dungeon populated with a multitude of terrifying monsters. You will need courage, determination and a fair amount of luck if you are to survive all the traps and battles, and reach your goal – the inner-most chambers of the Warlock's domain.

1 84046 387 2

The Citadel of Chaos
Steve Jackson

Deep inside the Citadel of Chaos, the dread sorcerer Balthus Dire is plotting the downfall of the goodfolk of the Vale of Willow. His battle plans are laid, his awesome army equipped, and attack is surely imminent.

Summoned by a desperate plea for help, YOU are the Vale of Willow's only hope. As star pupil of the Grand Wizard of Yore and a master sorcerer yourself, you must strike at the very heart of Balthus Dire's nightmare world. Though you command many powerful spells, the quest may be deadly, for who knows what creatures lie in wait in the Citadel of Chaos?

1 84046 389 9

Deathtrap Dungeon
Ian Livingstone

Down in the dark twisting labyrinth of Fang, unknown horrors await you. Devised by the devilish mind of Baron Sukumvit, the labyrinth is riddled with fiendish traps and bloodthirsty monsters, which will test your skills almost beyond the limit of endurance.

Countless adventurers before you have taken up the challenge of the Trial of Champions and walked through the carved mouth of the labyrinth, never to be seen again. Should you come out of the labyrinth alive, you will be wealthy beyond your dreams. Do YOU dare enter?

1 84046 388 0

Creature of Havoc
Steve Jackson

Evil is festering in Trolltooth Pass. The necromancer Zharradan Marr is close to stealing the secrets of Elven magic which would make him invincible. Nothing could then prevent his legions of Chaos from taking over the whole of Allansia ...

But what do you know or care about all this? In this unique adventure, YOU are the Creature of Havoc, a monstrous beast with a taste for fighting. Ruled only by hunger and rage, you have no knowledge of your past or destiny. If you survive, you may begin to control your bestial nature and learn your true purpose, but success is by no means certain, for the traps and terrors of Trolltooth Pass are many ...

1 84046 391 0

City of Thieves
Ian Livingstone

Terror stalks the night as Zanbar Bone and his bloodthirsty Moon Dogs hold the prosperous town of Silverton to ransom. YOU are an adventurer, a sword for hire, and the merchants of Silverton turn to you in their hour of need.

Your mission takes you along the dark, twisting streets of Port Blacksand to seek the help of the wizard Nicodemus. But Blacksand is riddled with thieves, assassins and foul creatures. Should you survive, you must journey to the most terrible place of all – the tower stronghold of the Night Prince himself, Zanbar Bone!

1 84046 397 X

Crypt of the Sorcerer
Ian Livingstone

An ancient evil is stirring in the bowels of the earth, and the land is blighted. After being entombed for one hundred years, the necromancer Razaak has been re-awoken and is poised to fulfil his promise of death and tyranny. His army of undead are at large across Allansia bringing death and destruction to all who resist.

It is up to YOU to find the only weapon to which Razaak is vulnerable – his own magic sword! Only then might you survive the dangers that await you in his evil lair – the Crypt of the Sorcerer!

1 84046 396 1

House of Hell
Steve Jackson

Stranded miles from anywhere on a dark and stormy night, your only hope of refuge is the strange, ramshackle mansion you can see in the distance …

But entering the House of Hell hurls you into an adventure of spine-chilling and blood-curdling terror. The dangers of the torrential storm outside are nothing compared to the nightmarish creatures that await you within its gruesome walls.

Be warned! You must try to keep your fear under control – collect too many FEAR points and you will die of fright. Can you make it through the night without being scared – to death?

1 84046 417 8

Sorcery! 1: The Shamutanti Hills
Steve Jackson

Based on the best-selling Fighting Fantasy gamebook system, *The Shamutanti Hills* is Book One in Steve Jackson's *Sorcery!* series. Your epic quest will take you across the mysterious hills to the cityport of Kharé, but only if you outwit the creatures, traps and wizardry you encounter along the way.

Play as either a warrior or as a wizard. If you choose wizardry, your survival will depend on your knowledge of the *Sorcery! Spell Book*'s darkest secrets. With many other unique features to discover, *Sorcery!* is a true challenge for novice and veteran adventurers alike.

1 84046 430 5